SMALL GROUPS

Chandler Publications in
ANTHROPOLOGY AND SOCIOLOGY
LEONARD BROOM, *Editor*

SMALL GROUPS

SOME SOCIOLOGICAL PERSPECTIVES

by

Clovis R. Shepherd

NATIONAL TRAINING LABORATORIES,
NATIONAL EDUCATION ASSOCIATION

CHANDLER PUBLISHING COMPANY
An Intext Publisher · Scranton, Pennsylvania 18515

International Standard Book No. 0-8102-0206-9

Copyright © 1964 by Chandler Publishing Company

Library of Congress Catalog Card No. 64-22883

Printed in the United States of America

I-R-RI

Contents

Preface ix

1. *Introduction* 1

2. *Perspectives for Understanding* 9
   The Attitude of Everyday Life 9
      Personal Perspective • Routinization •
      Typifications
   The Scientific Attitude 14
      General Perspective • The Posture of Doubt •
      Typifications
   Conclusion 18

3. *The Art of Speculation: Small-Group Theory* . . . 21
   Field Theory 23
   Interaction Process Analysis 27
   Homans's System Theory 36
   Other Theories 41
      Homans • Thibaut and Kelley • Festinger •
      Kelman • Blau • Emotionality Theories
   Conclusion 54

4. *The State of Empirical Knowledge: Research Findings* .   58

   Similarity-Dissimilarity   59

   Conformity   70

   Authority   81

   Cohesion and Productivity   85

   Conclusion   96

5. *Interpretation, Prediction, and Control*   .   .   .   100

   Interpretation   105

   Prediction   110

   Control   117

   Conclusion   119

Appendix: Features of the Successful Group   .   .   .   122

Index   126

Abstracts of Literature

Newcomb, "The Prediction of Interpersonal Attraction,"
American Psychologist 11:575-586 63

Slater, "Role Differentiation in Small Groups," *American
Sociological Review* 20:300-310 67

Deutsch and Gerard, "A Study of Normative and Informational Social Influences upon Individual Judgment,"
Journal of Abnormal and Social Psychology 51:629-636   71

Schachter, "Deviation, Rejection, and Communication,"
Journal of Abnormal and Social Psychology 46:190-207   75

Dentler and Erikson, "The Functions of Deviance in
Groups," *Social Problems* 7:98-107 78

Whyte, "Corner Boys: A Study of Clique Behavior," *American Journal of Sociology* 46:647-664 83

Whyte, "The Social Structure of the Restaurant," *American Journal of Sociology* 54:302-310 86

Bavelas, "Communication Patterns in Task-Oriented Groups,"
Journal of the Acoustical Society of America 22:725-730   89

Schachter *et al.*, "An Experimental Study of Cohesiveness
and Productivity," *Human Relations* 4:229-238 . . 92

Preface

This book has two major purposes: (1) to introduce the reader to a selection of sociological and social-psychological theory and research dealing with the small group; and (2) to organize this material within the perspectives of pure and applied social science and within the philosophical positions of symbolic interactionism and positivism. The primary audiences I have had in mind in writing this book are college students beginning their studies in sociology and social psychology, and adults who, because of the nature of their jobs or because of their curiosity, are interested in the dynamics of interpersonal relations and small groups.

In order to achieve these two purposes I have stressed the importance of personal understanding. By personal understanding I mean perceiving events accurately and relating theories and research findings to what people experience or can potentially experience in their daily lives. I think too little attention has been paid to the fact that the social scientist is a human being and that the interpretations he makes of the data he collects are much more dependent on his personal understandings than is the case with physical scientists. Although it is true that greater agreement in interpretation among social scientists is possible as advances are made in theory and in measuring instruments, it is still true that the researcher's personality is inextricably bound up in the research process.

It is difficult for me to indicate all of the writers, teachers, colleagues, and students who have influenced my perspective, but some of them stand out in my mind as unusually influential. I have always been impressed by John Dewey's philosophy and his insistence that the individual must begin his learning from his own unique situation—this has led me to emphasize an inductive approach in this book and an understanding in personal terms, rather than in abstract terms alone. I have also been strongly influenced by George H. Mead's philosophy of symbolic interactionism and by Alfred H. Schutz's phenomenological approach to social life, which have led me to emphasize the individual's perspective in situations. Kurt Lewin's concern for understanding the behavior of persons in situations and George C. Homans's clarity of writing have been a more immediate influence, both on my perspective and on my writing style.

When I was a graduate student at the University of California, Los Angeles, I was much impressed by the methodological approaches of Leonard Broom, Richard T. Morris, and William H. Robinson, and am indebted to them for conveying to me an insistence on operational definitions of terms, and on the dynamic interplay of abstract thought and factual evidence. I am deeply indebted to the members of the Human Relations Research Group, Institute of Industrial Relations, U.C.L.A., for the opportunity to be a graduate research assistant and a colleague of theirs during most of my graduate work there. This small group of Paula Brown, Arnold Gebel, Verne Kallejian, Fred Massarik, Robert Tannenbaum, the late Irving R. Weschler, and myself (the make-up of the group during most of my stay) convinced me that a work group could be highly productive and, at the same time, devote a great deal of attention to its own internal dynamics.

In the last few years, the opportunity to be an intern with the National Training Laboratories, National Education Association, and to be a staff member of training programs in human relations and sensitivity training conducted by the Institute of Industrial Relations and by University Extension, both at U.C.L.A., have led me to be more interested in applied social science and in somehow combining what are often referred to as the humanistic and the scientistic traditions.

In writing this book I am indebted to Leonard Broom, editor of the Chandler Series in Anthropology and Sociology, for editorial wisdom—I am now thoroughly convinced that editors are the unsung heroes of academic writing.

My wife, Pat, has been a perpetual source of stimulation, challenge, encouragement, and secretarial help, and has once again demonstrated the importance of an intimate human relationship.

C. R. S.

University of California, Santa Barbara
December, 1963

SMALL GROUPS

Chapter 1

Introduction

The study of small groups is one of the major areas of current research in sociology and social psychology.[1] It is a field in which there is an abundance of research, there are continuing efforts to construct rigorous theories, there are promising attempts to apply mathematical models to theories and to research findings, and there are concerns with the application of findings to problems of daily life.

The small group is an essential mechanism of socialization and a primary source of social order. There is little doubt that a small group provides the major source of the values and attitudes people have, and an important source of pressures to conform to social values and attitudes. There is also little doubt that the roles which children learn within the family and the play group serve as the initial roles which they take into other situations. The small group serves an important mediating function between the individual and the larger society.[2]

The small group is utilized as an effective medium for a variety of purposes. Psychiatrists and clinical psychologists find group therapy[3] a promising addition to individual therapy. The

---

[1] In the most recent survey of small-group research, 1385 articles and books have been referenced, most of which have been published since the mid-1950's. See A. Paul Hare, *Handbook of Small Group Research* (New York: The Free Press of Glencoe, 1962).

[2] Leonard Broom and Philip Selznick, *Sociology* (3d ed., New York: Harper and Row, 1963), pp. 135-175.

[3] George R. Bach, *Intensive Group Psychotherapy* (New York: Ronald,

T-group or sensitivity-training group[4] is a major focus of training in human relations for supervisors, managers, leaders, and others. The small class is considered essential to a good educational program. Governing boards of various organizations use committees and subcommittees to do much of their work.[5] Social workers argue that treatment directed at the gang or the family offers hope in controlling delinquency.[6] The success of the Chinese Communists during the Korean War in controlling American prisoners-of-war is partly attributed to their use of small groups as a medium for self-criticism.[7]

It is relatively easy to appreciate the importance of the small group but much more difficult to define exactly what it is. A first approximation to a definition of a small group is that it is *two or more people interacting*. If we accept this definition without qualification we may have in mind many situations which have little in common with each other, such as a conversation between a person and a telephone operator (two persons inter-

---

1954), especially Chapters 1 and 2; Eric Berne, *Transactional Analysis in Psychotherapy* (New York: Grove, 1961).

[4] Warren G. Bennis, Kenneth D. Benne, and Robert Chin (eds.), *The Planning of Change* (New York: Holt, Rinehart, and Winston, 1961), especially Chapters 2, 6, 11, and 12; Irving R. Weschler and Jerome Reisel, *Inside a Sensitivity Training Group*, Industrial Relations Monograph No. 4 (Los Angeles: Institute of Industrial Relations, University of California); Chris Argyris, *Interpersonal Competence and Organizational Effectiveness* (Homewood, Ill.: Dorsey Press, 1962).

[5] For example, The Regents of the University of California, a governing board of sixteen appointed members and eight *ex officio* members, conduct much of their work through permanent and temporary committees, with the entire board meeting to receive reports and to make policy decisions and recommendations. At a three-day meeting, the first two days may be spent in committee meetings, and only the last day spent in a meeting of the board as a whole.

[6] For an example of the importance of group factors, see Rita Volkman and Donald R. Cressey, "Differential Association and the Rehabilitation of Drug Addicts," *American Journal of Sociology*, 69, 1963, pp. 129-142.

[7] Edgar H. Schein, "The Chinese Indoctrination Program for Prisoners of War," *Psychiatry*, 19, 1956, pp. 149-172; ——, "Interpersonal Communication, Group Solidarity, and Social Influence," *Sociometry*, 23, 1960, pp. 148-161.

acting) or the behavior of the employees of some large manufacturing plant (people interacting). The criteria we use to qualify the definition of a small group will have to be arbitrary because there is no widespread agreement among students of small groups on the relevant criteria. However, the criteria presented here are generally acceptable.

One qualification which can be made is that the small group as a type of social phenomenon is more organized and more enduring than a social relation or what Goffman has called a "focused gathering,"[8] but less organized and probably less enduring than a formal organization.[9] Goffman speaks of a focused gathering as a casual or informal meeting of several people for some purpose which is not expected to be a continuing activity. Illustrations of focused gatherings include parties, bridge games, house warmings, and similar events where several people gather for some purpose but where those attending do not intend to meet periodically for the same purpose. A social relation is any situation involving two or more interacting persons.

A formal organization is more structured than a small group, containing members some of whom know each other only by acquaintance (if at all) and divided into enduring subgroups, either by official design or by unofficial development. Some formal organizations are highly structured (a manufacturing plant, the Congress of the United States, a chain of supermarkets) while others are less structured (a church, a Masonic lodge, a club).

A second qualification is that small groups of two or three persons possess characteristics due to their size which are sharply modified or tend to disappear in groups of four or more. For example, in a two-person group, sentiments and feelings tend to be more emphasized than in larger groups,[10] and in a three-

[8] Erving Goffman, *Encounters* (Indianapolis: Bobbs-Merrill, 1961), pp. 7-14.

[9] Chris Argyris, *op. cit.* in note 4, especially Chapters 1 and 2.

[10] A. Paul Hare, *op. cit.* in note 1, pp. 240-242; Howard Becker and Ruth H. Useem, "Sociological Analysis of the Dyad," *American Sociological Review*, 7, 1942, pp. 13-26; Georg Simmel, "The Number of Members as

person group coalitions of two against one tend to be so potent and enticing that other characteristics of a small group may not be developed.[11] Because of these and related considerations, the greater portion of the discussion throughout this book will be most directly meaningful with reference to small groups of four or more members.

A third qualification is that as a small group increases in size it reaches some upper limit where the group seems to become altered so that its members establish formal rules and regulations and the group becomes more like a formal organization than a small group. It is difficult to specify this upper limit exactly, but most of the small groups which have been studied in the field and in the laboratory have had no more than twenty members and usually fewer than fifteen. For example, students of committees as work groups note that the most common sizes are five, seven, or nine;[12] applied social scientists using the sensitivity-training group, T-group, or discussion group in human-relations laboratories and management training prefer to limit the size to around fifteen as the upper limit; and supervisors or managers rarely have more than eight or ten immediate subordinates.[13]

These typical upper limits are exceeded in some cases and their significance is not as adequately understood as the significance of a group of only two or three persons. For our purposes in this book an adequate criterion is that a group be large

Determining the Sociological Form of the Group," I and II, *American Journal of Sociology*, 8, 1902, pp. 1-46 and 158-196.

[11] A. Paul Hare, *op. cit.* in note 1, pp. 242-243; Simmel, *op. cit.* in note 10; William A. Gamson, "Experimental Test of a Theory of Coalition Formation," *American Sociological Review*, 26, 1961, pp. 565-573.

[12] John James, "A Preliminary Study of the Size Determinant in Small Group Interaction," *American Sociological Review*, 16, 1951, pp. 474-477; ———, "The Distribution of Free-forming Small Group Size," *American Sociological Review*, 18, 1953, pp. 569-570; Robert F. Bales and Edgar F. Borgatta, "Size of Group as a Factor in the Interaction Profile," in A. Paul Hare, Edgar F. Borgatta, and Robert F. Bales (eds.), *Small Groups* (New York: Knopf, 1955), pp. 396-413.

[13] Lyndall Urwick, "The Manager's Span of Control," *Harvard Business Review*, May-June 1956, p. 39.

enough for group characteristics to develop and become stable, but small enough so that the members feel a sense of common identity and mutual awareness. In most cases the kind of group discussed in this book will have at least four members and will be small enough to share a common table.[14]

The fourth qualification is that a small group possesses some general characteristics to which attention is directed. The presence of group characteristics is readily agreed upon but their nature is not. For this reason, any set of group characteristics selected is somewhat arbitrary. The general characteristics of a small group to be emphasized in this book are common objectives (purposes or goals), a stable differentiation of roles, shared values and norms, criteria for membership, and patterns of communication.[15] These general characteristics will be discussed throughout the book and not under separate topical headings. Traditionally the small group has been called the primary group,[16] but the term primary has some connotations which suggest a primary group is only one type of small group, and other connotations which suggest that a small community can be treated as a primary group.[17]

In order to study the small group it is necessary to clarify two attitudes of social life which are relevant to an understanding both of experiences in small groups in daily life and also of the theory and research literature of scientific studies of small groups. Chapter 2 discusses the attitude of daily life and contrasts it

[14] Robert Bierstedt considers sharing a common table to be an important index of similarity (he calls it the alimentary index). See his *The Social Order* (2d ed.; New York: McGraw-Hill, 1963), pp. 459-460.

[15] For other descriptions see A. Paul Hare, *op. cit.* in note 1, pp. 9-10; Michael S. Olmsted, *The Small Group* (New York: Random House, 1959), Chapter II; Robert T. Golembiewski, *The Small Group* (Chicago: University of Chicago Press, 1962), Chapters I and II.

[16] Ellsworth Faris, "The Primary Group: Essence and Accident," *American Journal of Sociology*, 28, 1932, pp. 41-50; Edward A. Shils, "The Study of the Primary Group," Harold D. Lasswell and Daniel Lerner (eds.), *The Policy Sciences* (Palo Alto: Stanford University Press, 1951), pp. 44-69.

[17] Robert Redfield, *The Primitive World and Its Transformations* (Ithaca, N.Y.: Cornell University Press, 1957).

with the scientific attitude. It is important that the reader understand the perspective (attitude) with which the social scientist approaches the study of small groups so that he may better evaluate theory and research. It is also important that the reader understand the perspective with which people in daily life approach situations and interpret events so that he may better evaluate the usefulness of theories and research findings in interpreting and predicting behavior. These contrasts are important to keep in mind because people are so involved in small groups that it is difficult to be objective in studying them.

In Chapter 3, three general theories and several middle-range (limited) theories are presented to acquaint the reader with concepts to use in understanding behavior in small groups. Next, a chapter is devoted to a survey of the findings of research on small groups. The reader should find it desirable to work back and forth between these two chapters (Chapters 3 and 4) in order to develop his deductive and inductive reasoning. A good theory can be used to organize numerous research findings, and good research can be generalized. Scientific advance comes as theories are developed which can embrace more research findings and as research is conducted which can answer problems more general than that in the research setting itself.

Finally, Chapter 5 is devoted to the application of knowledge about small groups. A number of questions are raised and some answers are suggested. It is my intention as author that this discussion will stimulate the reader to apply the theories and findings of small-group research and to concern himself with the unanswered problems in the field.

Wherever possible I have cited recent and readily available works to document the ideas presented, and have tried to select those articles and books which deal with major issues and which are written in a style more readily comprehended by a diverse readership. Thus I have cited books on applied social science, leading textbooks in sociology and social psychology, and articles reprinted in the Bobbs-Merrill Reprint Series in the Social

Sciences. It is my intention that this procedure will enable both the teacher and the student to relate the ideas in this book to broader concerns in social psychology and sociology, and to supplement this book in whatever direction may be desired.

Selected Bibliography for Chapter 1

The student beginning his study of small groups should read the following four articles and three books as his first systematic introduction to the literature on small groups.

ARTICLES

Robert F. Bales, "Small-Group Theory and Research," in Robert K. Merton, Leonard Broom, and Leonard S. Cottrell, Jr. (eds.), *Sociology Today* (New York: Basic Books, 1959), pp. 293-305. An appraisal of theory and research on small groups, emphasizing the problematical aspects of the field.

Omar K. Moore and Alan R. Anderson, "Some Puzzling Aspects of Social Interaction," in Joan H. Criswell, Herbert Solomon, and Patrick Suppes (eds.), *Mathematical Methods in Small Group Processes* (Stanford: Stanford University Press, 1962), pp. 232-249. A discussion of games and puzzles played in daily life and their counterparts in social science, particularly probability theory and games of strategy, suggesting that such activities are far removed from the nature of much social interaction and describing an alternative approach, called by the authors "dynamic autotelic responsive environments."

Edward A. Shils, "The Study of the Primary Group," in Harold D. Lasswell and Daniel Lerner (eds.), *The Policy Sciences* (Palo Alto: Stanford University Press, 1951). A reasoned assessment of approaches to and purposes in studying small groups, and some suggestions for the direction of small-group research.

Fred L. Strodtbeck, "The Case for the Study of Small Groups," *American Sociological Review*, 19, 1954, pp. 651-657. A brief history of interest in the small group, an assessment of current work, and an overview of the fourteen articles on small groups published in this issue of the *Review*.

BOOKS

C. P. Snow, *The Masters* (Garden City, N.Y.: Doubleday, 1959). A novel about a small group of professors at a Cambridge University college confronted with the necessity of electing a new Master. Character portrayals, interpersonal relations, and group structure and dynamics are vividly portrayed.

Frederic M. Thrasher, *The Gang* (Chicago: University of Chicago Press, 1927).

William F. Whyte, *Street Corner Society* (2d ed.; Chicago: University of Chicago Press, 1955).

These two books by Thrasher and Whyte contain many observations and conclusions which have since been supported by numerous field and laboratory studies.

Chapter 2

Perspectives for Understanding

THE ATTITUDE OF EVERYDAY LIFE[1]

The attitude of daily life refers to the perspective which people employ in their day-to-day activities. It provides people a background for understanding events, interpreting behavior, and predicting the course of affairs. This perspective may be described in a few propositions which capture some of the major aspects of it and sift out much of the disorderly or idiosyncratic. One of the major assumptions of the scientific approach to everyday life is that behavior is orderly or can be made to appear orderly, and this orderliness should be capable of being characterized in a few propositions.

The attitude of everyday life may be said to be characterized by at least three major propositions. First, that a person views the world about him from his *personal perspective,* not from a general perspective. Second, that a person is constrained to *routinize*

[1] The following discussions of the attitude of daily life and the scientific attitude are based primarily on the writings of Alfred Schutz and Harold Garfinkel. See Garfinkel, "The Rational Properties of Scientific and Common Sense Activities," *Behavioral Science,* 5, 1960, pp. 72-83; Schutz, "Common-Sense and Scientific Interpretation of Human Action," *Philosophy and Phenomenological Research,* 14, 1953, pp. 1-38; ——, "On Multiple Realities," *Philosophy and Phenomenological Research,* 5, 1945, pp. 533-575; ——, "Choosing Among Projects of Action," *Philosophy and Phenomenological Research,* 12, 1951, pp. 161-184; ——, "Making Music Together," *Social Research,* 18, 1951, pp. 76-97; ——, "The Social World and the Theory of Social Action," *Social Research,* 27, 1960, pp. 203-221.

the world about him. Third, that a person is engaged in a process of *typification*, a process of forming generalized judgments about the world about him.

In everyday life a person adopts a personal perspective and tends to feel that the world revolves around him, that he is the center of the universe. This egocentric attitude is modified by the ability to be perceptive of and sensitive to others.[2] Perceptiveness and sensitivity are limited by the personal perspective, for a person tends to see things which fit the world as he sees it—he can imaginatively put himself in others' shoes, but he still knows which shoes belong to him. This process of perceiving and interpreting events in terms of one's individualized perspective leads a person to see what he expects to see, to interpret events in familiar terms, and to reconstruct events as he now (after the event) thinks they must have been.

The personal perspective is a product of the interplay between the individual and social life. A person's perspective reflects the shared perspective of members of one or more groups or social relations in which he is or has been involved, or into which he hopes to enter.[3] His perspective may also reflect the perspective of historical individuals who have left a written record of their experiences and ideas (such as St. Thomas Aquinas, Confucius, or Aristotle) or of historical groups (such as the ancient Greeks, the Mayans, or the Cretans). Some of these sources of a person's perspective may be called *reference groups*,[4] to indicate those groups which the individual uses as a point of reference for his own perspective. Reference groups may be *membership groups* (a person's family, his bowling team, his professional association,

[2] Tamotsu Shibutani, "Reference Groups as Perspectives," *American Journal of Sociology*, 60, 1955, pp. 562-569; ——, *Society and Personality* (Englewood Cliffs, N.J.: Prentice-Hall, 1961), pp. 250-260; Renato Tagiuri and Luigi Petrullo (eds.), *Person Perception and Interpersonal Behavior* (Stanford: Stanford University Press, 1958).

[3] See Shibutani, "Reference Groups as Perspectives," *op. cit.* in note 2.

[4] Ralph H. Turner, "Role-Taking, Role Standpoint, and Reference-Group Behavior," *American Journal of Sociology*, 61, 1956, pp. 316-328.

his colleagues at work, his lodge, or his church) or *nonmembership groups* (the ancient Greeks, the Apostles of Jesus, the bowling team of which he hopes to become a member). Nonmembership reference groups may be groups in which a person could not possibly become a member or they may be groups in which he hopes to become a member. In any case, the idea is that a person's perspective is a product partly of his own inclinations and partly of his accepting what he takes to be the ideas and sentiments of others, whether these others be specific persons with whom he has a relationship, members of groups in which he is also a member or hopes to become a member, or persons or groups with whom he is unlikely to have any personal contact but with whose ideas and sentiments he is familiar.

The personal perspective is one of the major characteristics of the attitude of everyday life. The fact that a person can imaginatively put himself in another's place to some degree and feel that others can see his position and in some degree understand his feelings makes social life possible. But no one can fully appreciate another person's perspective, just as no one can really believe that someone else can truly understand his perspective.[5]

ROUTINIZATION

The second characteristic of the attitude of everyday life is the inevitability of routinization. People reduce to routine many of the numerous decisions they are confronted with daily in order to increase that part of their daily lives which they can take for granted, which they can assume to be predictable. It is necessary to keep in mind that predictability in everyday life is assumed and not scientifically proved, for it is based on plausibility. It is plausible at best because people often encounter something only once before they enmesh it in their routine daily life—they are not concerned about gathering evidence regarding its existence or its nature. Having encountered it once in common circumstances they take it for granted that they will encounter it again in very much the same form.

[5] See Shibutani, *op. cit.* in note 3; Schutz, "Common-Sense and Scientific Interpretation of Human Action," *op. cit.* in note 1.

The process of routinization is necessary for the existence of social life. It would be impossible to adopt a doubtful posture regarding everything encountered, for were people to do so they would be able to accomplish little more than the care of their basic physical needs.[6] Try an experiment, some day, of adopting a questioning posture—from the time you arise, try to take nothing for granted, including the existence of water in the pipes, the proper functioning of the faucet, the presence of your toothbrush where you last left it, the adequate functioning of your car, and all other things you encounter during the day. If you do so you will find that it takes much more time to process your daily routine and you will be so engaged in the immediate situation that you will not anticipate future events to any degree. Not having anticipated later events you will not have imaginatively rehearsed them and when you do encounter them you will probably not behave in a way as satisfactory as you would prefer.

Of course, routinization can be carried too far. In its extreme form it can become a deadening influence, a rigidity and compulsiveness which not only reduce effectiveness by limiting flexibility and adaptiveness but also reduce enjoyment by eliminating surprise. Most people balance routinization with a taste of surprise—they occasionally purposefully break up their routines, they are attracted to the unusual and to the unanticipated, and they sometimes actively search for surprise. Most people cherish the surprises they encounter—not too much surprise, however, for too much surprise pushes a person too far toward the other extreme. Too much surprise with too little routine leads to chaos and the disruption of daily life. People gear their lives to a balance of routine and surprise, sufficient routine to enable them to operate at the symbolic level of their choosing, and enough surprise to keep their spirits high.

TYPIFICATIONS

The third characteristic of daily life is the development of typifications. Obviously people cannot maintain a complete de-

[6] For example, the struggle for food and shelter among primitive peoples living in niggardly geographical environments, such as deserts and snow-covered areas.

piction of what they encounter, nor can they interact meaningfully with others unless they develop a generalized conception of what others are like and how they are likely to behave.[7] The typifications used by strangers are apt to be wrong, at times, because they use stereotypes and judgments about categories of people. The typifications used by friends are more apt to be accurate, because friends have more personal acquaintance with each other than strangers and are less likely to view each other as representatives of categories. Friends may err, though, because of the self-sustaining nature of typifications. People know their friends well enough to think they know what their friends intended to say and sometimes they are right. But a person may overlook the weaknesses and magnify the strengths of a friend, just as he may overlook the strengths and magnify the weaknesses of a stranger or an opponent.[8]

The typifications in daily life are not developed in order to test hypotheses in a scientific manner, but rather to serve people by helping to maintain their personal perspectives and their routines. Stereotypes (a major kind of typification) persist because they work, not always but often enough to satisfy most people within their attitudes of daily life. If a person were to think that his typifications were wrong, he would have to reorganize a good deal of his symbolic world and to question some of what he had taken for granted.[9]

These characteristics of the attitude of daily life serve the purposes of individuals who are confronted with an ongoing round

[7] Shibutani, *Society and Personality, op. cit.* in note 2, pp. 111-118; Harold J. Leavitt, *Managerial Psychology* (Chicago: University of Chicago Press, 1958), pp. 65-80, for a discussion of storage capacity and the necessity for successive levels of generalized conceptions in dealing with complex situations.

[8] Shibutani, *Society and Personality, op. cit.* in note 2, pp. 228-239; David Krech, Richard S. Crutchfield, and Egerton L. Ballachey, *Individual in Society* (New York: McGraw-Hill, 1962), pp. 51-65.

[9] Leon Festinger, *A Theory of Cognitive Dissonance* (Evanston, Ill.: Row, Peterson, 1957); Krech, Crutchfield, and Ballachey, *op. cit.* in note 8; Schutz, "Common-Sense," *op. cit.* in note 1; Shibutani, *Society and Personality, op. cit.* in note 2, Chapter 16 and 17.

of life and who must invest it with meaning consistent with expectations. People can have firsthand knowledge, at best, of only
a small portion of what affects them—this portion they see from
their own perspective. Much that is seen and done must be reduced to routine both to conserve energy and to satisfy others.
Finally, much of what affects people can only be known from a
distance—this portion must be typified as well as those things
which are experienced directly. The total of these characteristics
leads to multiple realities[10]—to a succession of multiple worlds in
which people must move and pretend to be knowledgeable; they
must also take at face value much of what is presented to them,
just as their associates must honor them by taking much of what
they present to others at face value. To do otherwise is to court
disaster—people cannot afford to question all the motivations of
others, much less of themselves. The sociologist interpreting daily
life might well subscribe to a sociological paraphrasing of
Occam's razor: First seek the explanation of events in observed,
manifest behavior; probe the underlying dynamics only if the
explanations are inadequate.

THE SCIENTIFIC ATTITUDE

The attitude of daily life cannot by itself lead to the development of scientific principles of human behavior, and any understanding sought in this attitude may not lead people far beyond
colloquial knowledge. In order to develop scientific knowledge
it is necessary to adopt a *scientific attitude* and, armed with this
perspective, to approach the study of daily life. The attitude
which the social scientist seeks to develop is characterized by a
general perspective, a posture of *doubt,* and *typifications.*

GENERAL PERSPECTIVE

The scientist seeks to develop a general perspective which will
enable him to escape from the limitations of the personal perspective. He is interested in things common to all people or to

[10] Schutz, "On Multiple Realities," *op. cit.* in note 1.

groups of people. He seeks to abstract from the personal perspectives those elements which are common and to discard those elements which are idiosyncratic. In adopting a general perspective the scientist confronts two methodological problems. First, he must control his own personal perspective by removing himself from the behavior he is studying.[11] By not being a participant in the group he is better able to control his personal biases and identifications and better able to understand the diverse personal perspectives of the participants. When he finds it necessary to be a participant, he seeks to adopt a neutral role to avoid involvement in the politics of the group.

Second, he must control the nature of the abstractions he makes from the personal perspectives of the participants by using standardized procedures (such as observer forms, questionnaires, and the like) and associates.[12] The standardized procedures help him avoid missing relevant things, and the associates help him check on the reliability of his observations and abstractions.

THE POSTURE OF DOUBT

The scientist must also reverse the routinization of daily life—he can afford to take nothing for granted except the basic assumptions of science.[13] In daily life the individual is led to question something he has taken for granted only after he encounters trouble, but in scientific research the scientist must question everything. Even when observations and abstractions are supported by a great deal of evidence, the scientist must still consider

[11] Ralph Ross, *Symbols and Civilization* (New York: Harcourt, 1962), and Peter L. Berger, *Invitation to Sociology: A Humanist Perspective* (Garden City, N.Y.: Doubleday, 1963) provide good introductions to the problem of the observer removing himself from what he studies.

[12] Herbert Hyman, *Survey Design and Analysis* (Glencoe, Ill.: Free Press, 1955), and Claire Selltiz, Marie Jahoda, Morton Deutsch, and Stuart W. Cook, *Research Methods in Social Relations* (revised one-volume edition; New York: Holt, 1959) provide good introductions to the use of standardized procedures and associates in improving reliability of observations.

[13] See Ross, *op. cit.* in note 11; Berger, *op. cit.* in note 11; Schutz, "Common-Sense and Scientific Interpretation of Human Action," *op. cit.* in note 1.

them open to disproof.[14] In everyday life people can hold on to
their attitudes and beliefs in the face of overwhelming contrary
evidence[15]—after all, it is a person's right and privilege to be
stubborn or stupid, and he is likely to find someone who agrees
with him. As long as someone else feels the same way, this support can go a long way in helping him maintain his position.

But a scientist who maintains a position in the face of overwhelming contrary evidence is due to be ridden out of the
professional fraternity. To be sure, the matter isn't quite this
simple—what constitutes "overwhelming contrary evidence" may
be a controversial matter. Raise the question of the existence of
extrasensory perception (ESP) in a gathering of psychologists or
sociologists and the fur is apt to fly. A few will defend its existence staunchly, a few more will admit there is probably something there to be explained, but most will question the existence
of unexplained phenomena. However, the one statement that they
are all likely to accept, even though grudgingly, is that the existence of ESP is not a closed matter and it would be foolish,
scientifically, to ignore it without taking a close look at the
evidence.[16]

The posture of doubt leads social scientists to question things
which people take for granted in everyday life, and to insist on
evidential proof of even the most rudimentary aspects of human
behavior. It is no longer necessary to caution many people that
some of the things they take for granted are culturally determined and vary from one culture to another (examples: forms of
greeting, foods, marriage customs, or the distance people maintain between themselves when conducting business or having a

[14] See Ross, *op. cit.* in note 11; Berger, *op. cit.* in note 11; Hans Reichenbach, *The Rise of Scientific Philosophy* (Berkeley and Los Angeles: University of California Press, 1951).

[15] Leon Festinger, Henry W. Riecken, Jr., and Stanley Schachter, *When
Prophecy Fails* (Minneapolis: University of Minnesota Press, 1956). In this
book the authors show how members of a religious sect maintain their
faith and their belief in the prophetic wisdom of their leader in the face
of a series of disconfirming evidences of the leader's prophecies.

[16] See, for example, Gardner Murphy, "Trends in the Study of Extrasensory Perception," *American Psychologist*, 13, 1958, pp. 69-76.

private talk[17]). It is more difficult, though, to convince people that they should be wary of accepting the wisdom of proverbs, sayings, or folk knowledge. Proverbs provide a basis for predicting the future and explaining the past, and almost any behavior can be predicted or explained by one or another proverb. Of a couple anticipating a separation of several months, one may console himself by thinking "absence makes the heart grow fonder," while the other is fearful because of thinking "out of sight, out of mind." Careful research will probably show that both of these sayings are right under some conditions and wrong under other conditions.

The goal of the scientist is to achieve the maximum possible accuracy in prediction—but prediction based on theory and research, not on one's personal preferences. The maximum possible accuracy in prediction is achieved by substituting scientific evidence for assumption and by testing the adequacy of explanation by the accuracy of prediction. For example, the assumption that absence makes the heart grow fonder would be questioned and data gathered to indicate whether, when people separate for a length of time, the separation leads to greater, lesser, or the same fondness for each other. Gathering data would become complex because the researcher would have to decide what is meant by fondness, what kinds of relations are involved (one would not equate lovers with friends or acquaintances), what kinds of separation exist, and other details. The researcher would also have to decide what other kind of information might make the answer to the question conditional. If both persons in a given case believe "out of sight, out of mind," this agreement might lead to a different result than would follow if both persons believe "absence makes the heart grow fonder." Once the researcher feels he has some evidence to justify the idea that, under some conditions, absence makes the heart grow fonder, he then must gather new data and predict this result in order to test the adequacy of his explanation.[18]

[17] See Clyde Kluckhohn, *Mirror For Man* (New York: McGraw-Hill, 1949).

[18] The distinction between *ex post facto* and predictive studies is very important. See Selltiz, *et. al., op. cit.* in note 12; Hyman, *op. cit.* in note 12.

TYPIFICATIONS

The scientist is engaged in developing typifications, but the typifications he develops differ from those in daily life in two major ways. First, they are typifications of typifications.[19] The raw data of the social scientist are the ideas and feelings of people in everyday life. What is perceived, thought, or felt by people is the reality of the social scientist's subject matter—if a person believes in ghosts and this belief affects his behavior, then the social scientist accepts "belief in ghosts" as reality. The scientist is more concerned with how this belief influences a person's behavior than whether ghosts exist or not. He suspects that if a person believes in ghosts he is not likely to change this belief very easily because within the attitude of daily life this belief may be desirable, meaningful, or necessary in order to maintain acceptance in a social group or to sustain a person's conception of himself or the world about him.

Second, the scientist's typifications are developed in order to serve a common goal with other social scientists, rather than to serve his own personal ends. He must follow certain rules in developing typifications in order for them to gain acceptance—otherwise, the typifications are suspect of being only his own personal preferences. The typifications must be consistent with what is taken to be the abstract nature of that part of human behavior comprised in his field, with what other people have found in research, and with the measuring instruments which are in use. The ability of scientists to repeat the studies of others and to reach the same conclusions is essential to the development of tested knowledge and to the sustaining of a general perspective.

CONCLUSION

The scientific attitude differs in many respects from the attitude of everyday life. Some of these differences are obvious,

---

[19] See Schutz, "Common Sense and Scientific Interpretation of Human Action," *op. cit.* in note 1, on the notion of typifications of typifications, especially on this point as an important distinction between social and physical science.

but many more are subtle and difficult to portray in a few sentences. A person within the attitude of daily life may function well or poorly in small groups but he cannot develop tested and testable propositions about behavior in small groups. If he desires to understand and be able to utilize the work of social scientists on small groups he will have to cultivate the scientific attitude. This attitude you must now assume and maintain as you take up the rest of this book. As you read the succeeding chapters and agree or disagree with what you read, you should ask yourself whether your reaction is based on your attitude of daily life or on your assumption of the scientific attitude. At first you will find it difficult to assume the scientific attitude, and as you master this ability you will probably find yourself assuming one attitude or the other exclusively at different times. It is possible to develop an ability to shift perspectives easily, and this ability is necessary if you are to relate scientific study on small groups to your experiences, and to utilize scientific knowledge about small groups in the conduct of your daily life.

An underlying assumption of this book is that much more is known scientifically about human behavior than is put into practice, and it is my conviction that this difference is largely due to a failure to understand the difference between the attitude of daily life and the scientific attitude and to develop the ability to shift perspectives. The emphasis on personal understandings embodied in this book is designed to help solve these two failures and to encourage a closer relationship between "pure" and applied social science.

Selected Bibliography for Chapter 2

ARTICLES

Abraham Kaplan, "Sociology Learns the Language of Mathematics," in James R. Newman (ed.), *The World of Mathematics, Volume Two* (New York: Simon and Schuster, 1956), pp. 1294-1313. A discussion of promising leads and disappointing results in attempts to apply mathematical models to social behavior.

Alfred Schutz, especially "Common-Sense and Scientific Interpretation of Human Action," *Philosophy and Phenomenological Research,* 5, 1945, pp. 533-575; and "Choosing Among Projects of Action," *Philosophy and Phenomenological Research,* 12, 1951, pp. 161-184; see also footnote 1, this chapter. The work of Alfred Schutz follows in the phenomenological heritage of German philosophers and bears a close resemblance in many ways to the American tradition in sociology and social psychology stemming from the works of George H. Mead and Charles H. Cooley.

BOOKS

Peter Berger, *Invitation to Sociology: A Humanist Perspective* (Garden City, N.Y.: Doubleday, 1963). A readable and knowledgeable introduction to the sociological perspective.

Abraham Kaplan, *The Conduct of Inquiry* (San Francisco: Chandler, 1964). A penetrating and wide-ranging analysis of methodological problems in behavioral science.

Ralph Ross, *Symbols and Civilization* (New York: Harcourt, 1962). A discussion of the role of symbols in thought, logical analysis, science, and society.

Chapter 3

The Art of Speculation: Small-Group Theory

When a person adopts the scientific attitude he finds it necessary to learn a new vocabulary of assumptions and concepts (typifications of typifications), to familiarize himself with the methods and findings of research, and to concern himself with advancing and applying scientific knowledge. In this chapter a vocabulary is presented, drawing on some of the more frequently cited theories about small groups. Chapter 4 will take up the methods and findings of research on small groups, and Chapter 5 deals with advancing and applying scientific knowledge about small groups.

The vocabulary of the sociology of small groups (as of any scientific field) consists primarily of three kinds of *words*, variables, constructs, and concepts, and two kinds of *statements*, assumptions and hypotheses.[1] A *variable* describes phenomena which take on varying values and which may be very general or

---

[1] See Paul F. Lazarsfeld, "Problems in Methodology," in Robert K. Merton, Leonard Broom, and Leonard S. Cottrell, Jr. (eds.), *Sociology Today* (New York: Basic Books, 1959); Hans Zetterberg, "On Axiomatic Theories in Sociology," in Paul F. Lazarsfeld and Morris Rosenberg (eds.), *The Language of Social Research* (Glencoe, Ill.: Free Press, 1955), pp. 533-540; Allen H. Barton, "The Concept of Property-Space in Social Research," in Lazarsfeld and Rosenberg, *ibid.*, pp. 40-57; W. S. Robinson, "The Logical Structure of Analytic Induction," *American Sociological Review*, 16, 1951, pp. 812-818; Ralph H. Turner, "The Quest for Universals in Sociological Research," *American Sociological Review*, 18, 1953, pp. 604-611.

very specific. A *construct* is one type of variable which describes an abstract and complex quality of small groups, not directly observable itself. A construct is a logical tool, a part of a theory. A *concept* is a second type of variable which may be relatively complex or simple but which is operationalized (at least partly), that is, which describes directly or indirectly observable phenomena.

A commonly used variable in the study of small groups is *interaction*. As a construct, interaction may refer to the process of acting and reacting which takes place between people meeting together in a small group. It is abstract and complex because it includes what is manifestly and subliminally communicated between people, what is intended and what is expressed, how messages are interpreted, and the like. As a concept, interaction may refer to the overt expressions of persons meeting together in a small group, specifically to the words and gestures which are used and their apparent meaning both to the communicator and to the interpreter. A concept may or may not be related to a construct, and it may consist of several specific variables averaged together in some way or of only one specific variable. For example, the concept of interaction could be measured by averaging together the variables of number and kind of words directed at each other by two persons, number of gestures directed at each other, and subjective recall of attention paid to each other; or interaction could be measured only by one of these three variables.

An *assumption* is a statement whose truth or correctness is not questioned in the immediate use. Such statements might be the assumptions that people behave so as to avoid punishment and to gain rewards, that they have a need to affiliate with others, or that they seek to be liked and have their behavior approved. A *hypothesis* is a statement indicating how two or more constructs or concepts are related to each other, and is subject to being found true or false by research. An example of a hypothesis might be "the greater the interaction among members of a group, the greater the cohesion of a group." This statement is capable of being found true or false by gathering information on interaction and cohesion of members of a group over time, or on several groups at one point in time, testing to see whether these two concepts (or, in fact, the variables used as indicators of the concepts) do vary systematically with each other as predicted by the hypothesis.

A *theory* is a set of constructs, concepts, variables, assumptions, and hypotheses which is intended to organize the available scientific knowledge dealing with some topic and to guide further research. Without a theory of some kind a researcher is unable to do much more than he does in the course of his daily life. If a researcher in using a given theory finds it difficult or impossible to relate the theory to what he can observe, if he finds the hypotheses or the theory refuted by the evidence he gathers, or if he finds the theory incapable of satisfactorily organizing available knowledge, he is likely to discard that theory and use another theory or develop one (or parts of one).

The development and use of a theory involves some of the qualities of artistic activity (it is imaginative and expressive) and of speculation (it is contemplative and risky).[2] The art of speculation refers to the scientist's theoretical work, to his selection and use of constructs, concepts, variables, assumptions, and hypotheses, and to the underlying skills of logical analysis and intuition.

Three theories about small groups are discussed in detail below. The chapter concludes with brief comments on several other small-group theories and with some general comments on small-group theory and research. The three theories to be discussed in detail are field theory as developed by the late Kurt Lewin, and two system theories as developed by George C. Homans and Robert Freed Bales.

FIELD THEORY

Field theory[3] (or group dynamics as it is often called) has been

[2] The artist creates a picture, a symphony, or a sculpture, just as the theorist creates a set of ideas.
[3] Kurt Lewin, "Frontiers in Group Dynamics," *Human Relations,* 1, 1947,

highly influential among social psychologists (both psychologists and sociologists) for a quarter of a century. Field theory as applied to small groups is generally attributed to Kurt Lewin, and even though it has been modified since Lewin's early formulations his analysis still serves as an excellent introduction.

The influence of Lewin is due to three major factors: First, his basic commitment to a *phenomenological position* which, in the nineteen thirties, was rare in psychology. This position is a remarkably simple and plausible one, and is eminently satisfactory to sociologists. Lewin argued that the phenomena to which the psychologist should direct his attention are what the individual subjectively perceives, not what the observer perceives as the "objective reality." Thus the source of social-psychological phenomena is held to be in the person, and not in the environment. Second, his *ingenuity in research design*. The study on leadership climate (in which the effect of three different styles of leadership on three different groups of children is studied) is a classic in research design and in findings. This ingenuity led Lewin to investigate phenomena which had largely been ignored, and established the viability of the laboratory as a setting for important human research. And, third, his *theoretical system*, which he attempted to represent mathematically by utilizing topology (a type of nonquantitative geometry).

Lewin's art of speculation begins by developing a conceptual system of the individual which, later, is applied to the small group. Underlying his theory is a series of five assumptions, including: (1) that the phenomena to be studied are what the individual perceives in his environment; this assumption leads to the concept of the *psychological field* or *life space* of the individual; (2) that a person occupies a *position* in this life space which is related (near or distant) to the objects of which it is comprised; (3) that a person is oriented toward *goals*, which ordinarily involve a change in the relative positions of the individual and the objects in the life space; (4) that the individual behaves in certain ways

---

pp. 5-41 and 143-153; —— (Dorwin Cartwright, ed.), *Field Theory in Social Science* (New York: Harper, 1951).

to achieve these goals, or *locomotes;* and (5) that in the process of locomotion toward goals the individual may encounter *barriers* which have to be surmounted or circumvented, or which may result in a change in goals or in life space or in both. These assumptions and the key concepts embodied in them constitute a methodology which serves as the foundation for Lewin's theoretical formulations and constitutes the major contribution of field theory to the art of speculation. The theoretical contributions of Lewin constitute largely a series of hypotheses dealing with certain specific problems rather than an over-all theory of behavior.

The field-theory approach is applied to groups through substituting the term "group" for the term "individual." A group has a life space, it occupies a position relative to other objects in this life space, it is oriented toward goals, it locomotes in pursuit of these goals, and it may encounter barriers in the process of locomotion. In applying the scheme to groups, the field theorist finds it necessary to introduce new concepts to deal with certain other realities of groups: *norms,* referring to the rules governing behavior of members of the group; *roles,* especially leadership, referring to the relative status and prestige of members and to their rights and duties as members of the group; *power* and *influence,* referring to the kind and amount of control that members have over each other; and *cohesion,* referring to the degree of attachment (involvement, belongingness, importance) that members have for the group. Several subsidiary concepts are utilized, such as *valence,* indicating the potency of goals or of objects in the life space; *interaction,* the type and degree of communication between members; and *consensus,* the degree of agreement regarding goals, norms, roles, and other aspects of the group.

The field theorist expands the conceptual scheme to deal adequately with the nature of groups, and in so doing modifies the scheme rather significantly. So significantly, in fact, that one of the primary foci of field theorists in the study of small groups has been cohesion and its relation to various other aspects of group behavior, such as style of leadership, productivity, interaction, influence, and other topics. Hence it would be reasonable to argue that the key concept of field theory of small groups is that of cohesion, and that this emphasis represents a significant departure from field theory of individuals, for whom the key concept is life space. The other concepts are utilized and a field theorist in analyzing the group is interested in the overlap of member life spaces—but these concepts tend to take a secondary place to cohesion as the methodological and theoretical focus.

The field theorist, in applying his approach to the analysis of small groups, then, is essentially concerned with cohesion. In the analysis of cohesion he is primarily interested in two sets of concepts: (1) those which tend to produce or be associated with greater or lesser cohesion, such as agreement on goals and understandings, on role differentiation, on norms; and (2) those which tend to be the effects or products of cohesion, such as interaction patterns, productivity, satisfaction, and influence.

The concept of cohesion refers basically to the complex of forces which bind members of a group to each other and to the group as a whole. These forces include the satisfactions members obtain from being in a group, the degree of closeness and warmth they feel for each other, the pride they feel from being members of a group, the ability they have to meet emergencies and crises which may confront them as a group, and their willingness to be frank and honest in their expression of ideas and feelings. A key indicator of group cohesion is the way in which a group makes a decision: where the members make a decision by acquiescence to the leader or by a majority vote, cohesion is probably low; where the members make a decision by unanimity, especially where this unanimity means that all members feel they have had their say and that even though they may still have reservations they are personally willing to express agreement, cohesion is probably high.

Some of the major propositions or hypotheses of field theorists which have been subjected to research include the following: (1) cohesion is directly related to agreement on goals, agreement on norms, extent of democratic and stable leadership, agreement on shared understandings, and similarity in background (age, experience, ethnic identification, and the like); and (2) cohesion is directly related to productivity, satisfaction, conformity (and influence), and cooperative interaction patterns. These propositions are not precise statements of hypotheses nor exhaustive of the hypotheses subjected to research or derivable from theory, but they indicate the general nature of the direction of theoretical analysis and research which have been conducted by field theorists, especially by the first generation of Lewin's students.[4]

INTERACTION PROCESS ANALYSIS

Lewin's field theory is a perspective that has excited social psychologists because it is challenging, theoretically simple, and its use has led to empirical research. A major focus of field theory has been the individual and his relation to the group, with less attention to the characteristics of the group itself. A second theory which has placed more emphasis on the group and less on the individual has been the theory and observational scheme of Robert F. Bales.[5] Bales's interaction process analysis (IPA) has had a considerable impact on the study of small groups, though for different reasons and with different consequences than Lewin's field theory. Where Lewin draws on the psychology of the individual for his point of departure, Bales draws on the sociology of groups and social systems, and where Lewin's major contribution is an over-all perspective, Bales's major contribution is an observational scheme.

[4] Dorwin Cartwright, "Achieving Change in People," *Human Relations,* 4, 1951, pp. 381-392; —— and Ronald Lippitt, "Group Dynamics and the Individual," *International Journal of Psychotherapy,* 7, 1957, pp. 86-102; —— and Alvin Zander (eds.), *Group Dynamics* (2d ed.; Evanston, Ill.: Row, Peterson, 1960), especially Chapters 1, 2, 3, 9, 19, 25, 34.

[5] Robert F. Bales, *Interaction Process Analysis* (Cambridge, Mass.: Addison-Wesley, 1950); ——, "A Set of Categories for the Analysis of Small Group Interaction," *American Sociological Review,* 15, 1950, pp. 257-263; ——, "In Conference," *Harvard Business Review,* 32, 1954, pp. 44-50; ——, "How People Interact in Conference," *Scientific American,* CXCII, 1955, pp. 31-35; ——, "Small-Group Theory and Research," in Robert K. Merton, Leonard Broom, and Leonard S. Cottrell, Jr., *Sociology Today* (New York: Basic Books, 1959).

The observational scheme is closely articulated to a conceptual analysis, a feature which gives IPA a quality of challenge, theoretical simplicity, and research usefulness comparable to field theory. The cogency of IPA is attested by its continued use in group research and its ability to encompass interpretations based on alternative theories, including field theory.

The conceptual analysis involves basically a consideration of four main problems with which a small group is confronted. These problems are, respectively, *adaptation* to factors outside the group which influence the group (for example, control by a larger organization of which the group is a member or necessity to cooperate with another group); *instrumental control* over those things in the group which are relevant to performing its work (for example, assigning tasks, making decisions, or performing activities); the *expression and management of feelings* of the members (for example, expressing dissatisfaction or pleasure, resolving interpersonal antagonisms, or relieving tensions); and the *development and maintenance of integration* of the members with each other and of the group as a whole (for example, willingness to do things, satisfaction with the group, or a sense of comradeship).

The problems of adaptation and instrumental control are handled primarily by the expression of questions and answers. Information, opinions, and suggestions are requested and offered by group members as they attempt to orient themselves to task problems they are confronted with, evaluate information and suggestions, and decide what to do. The problems of the expression and management of feelings and the development and maintenance of integration are dealt with largely by the expression of positive and negative reactions. As group members interact they express agreement or disagreement with each other and with decisions they are making; they display tension or tension release as they feel interested, bored, satisfied, or disturbed; and they show solidarity or antagonism as they feel a sense of (or lack of) integration, helpfulness to each other, or friendliness.

On the basis of a conceptual analysis of problems confronting a group and an analysis of statements made by and behavior exhibited by members of small discussion groups, Bales developed a classification of communicative acts which is used as a scheme for observing a group. This classification scheme is outlined in Table 1, where distinctions are made between four major categories of communicative acts, twelve subcategories (in four sets of three, each set corresponding to one major category), and some illustrative statements of behavior representing each of the subcategories.

The key concept in the use of the category system as an observational scheme is the unit "act." Bales and others using IPA have defined *act* as verbal and nonverbal behavior of a person which is communicated to at least one other person in the group and which has an observable beginning and end. Some acts may be short, others long. Ordinarily, one complete sentence or an independent phrase is considered an act, though several sentences could be lumped together as one act if their import were essentially the same. More common than this latter, however, might be the categorization of a sentence, phrase, or word in one category and the accompanying expression of feeling in another category. Typically, each sentence or independent phrase would be scored as one act, so that a person's comment could be scored as several acts of communication or as only one act. Each act would be scored in three ways: as to who originates the act, as to the nature of the act, and as toward whom the act is directed. In addition, a temporal sequence of acts can be noted, so that in the end an observer can have a record of who said what, to whom, when, and what the reaction was.

It is obvious that one observer watching six persons in a meeting may well have his hands full in trying to catch all acts and record them. He must have the scheme firmly fixed in his mind and he must have a device for recording acts rapidly. He cannot afford to miss much, nor can he afford to place an act in the wrong category or note the wrong person engaging in the act or

Table 1

INTERACTION PROCESS ANALYSIS, CATEGORIES OF COMMUNICATIVE ACTS*

Major Categories	Subcategories	Illustrative Statements or Behavior
A. POSITIVE REACTIONS	a. SHOWS SOLIDARITY b. SHOWS TENSION RELEASE c. SHOWS AGREEMENT	Jokes, gives help, rewards others, is friendly Laughs, shows satisfaction, is relieved Passively accepts, understands, concurs, complies
B. ANSWERS	d. GIVES SUGGESTION e. GIVES OPINION f. GIVES INFORMATION	Directs, suggests, implies autonomy for others Evaluates, analyzes, expresses feeling or wish Orients, repeats, clarifies, confirms
C. QUESTIONS	g. ASKS FOR INFORMATION h. ASKS FOR OPINION i. ASKS FOR SUGGESTION	Requests orientation, repetition, confirmation Requests evaluation, analysis, expression of feeling or wish Requests direction, possible ways of action
D. NEGATIVE REACTIONS	j. SHOWS DISAGREEMENT k. SHOWS TENSION l. SHOWS ANTAGONISM	Passively rejects, resorts to formality, withholds help Asks for help, withdraws, daydreams Deflates other's status, defends or asserts self, is hostile

* Based on Robert F. Bales, *Interaction Process Analysis*, and on A. Paul Hare, *Handbook of Small Group Research*, p. 66. Terminology modified slightly.

the wrong person toward whom the act is directed. Training in observation can produce satisfactory reliability, and supplementary use of tape recorders, movies, or both can aid the procedure. There is even some indication that scoring from a recorded or written protocol without direct observation of a group can produce satisfactory reliability. However, training in scoring and observation is essential, even if one uses only the four major categories (positive reactions, questions, answers, and negative reactions). It is not easy, but it is feasible, so that the reliability of the scheme can be made satisfactorily high.

For the findings of research using the IPA scheme it will be adequate to draw on the major points Bales makes in two popular articles.[6] It is important to note that most of the research which has utilized IPA has been conducted with problem-solving groups composed, for the most part, of college students. There is good reason to believe, however, that the nature and distribution of acts does not vary radically with different normal populations, so that these findings can be applied (generalized) to problem-solving groups of people generally.

With this reservation in mind we can turn to the specific findings. First, the distribution of acts by category provides a useful portrait of the behavior of members of a group. On the basis of published profiles, this distribution averages about 25 per cent in positive reactions, 56 per cent in answers, 7 per cent in questions, and 12 per cent in negative reactions. Thus about half of the communicative acts of a group constitute answers, and the other half is distributed among positive reactions, negative reactions, and questions, in that order. Furthermore, there are about twice as many positive reactions as negative reactions. Within each of these four broad areas, the distribution breakdown, on the average, is: within answers, most acts are expressions of *opinions* and *information;* within positive reactions, most acts are expressions of *agreement,* some of *tension release,* with very few expressions

---

[6] Robert F. Bales, "In Conference," *op. cit.* in note 5; ——, "How People Interact in Conferences," *op. cit.* in note 5.

of *solidarity;* within negative reactions, most acts are expressions of *disagreement;* and within questions, most acts are requests for *information* or *opinion.* The portrait, then, is of a group in which most of the discussion involves expressing *opinions* and *information* and conveying *agreement,* with occasional expressions of *disagreement* and *tension release* (such as joking) and occasional requests for *information* and *opinion.*

Satisfied and dissatisfied groups differ somewhat in their profiles. In general, there is very little difference in the percentage of answers, though in satisfied groups there are about twice as many suggestions and fewer requests for orientation than in dissatisfied groups. But the striking profile differences occur in positive and negative reactions, where dissatisfied groups have about three times as much disagreement and only about one-third as much agreement as satisfied groups. The major variation in communicative acts among groups appears to be in the areas of positive and negative reactions, rather than in answers and questions. This interpretation is supported by Philp and Dunphy[7] in a study of student groups at the University of Sydney in which they found greater variation among their groups in positive and negative reactions than in answers and questions. It is interesting to note that Philp and Dunphy also found that Sydney students tended to express a greater percentage of questions and lesser percentages of positive and negative reactions than American students.

There is also a variation in the ratio of instrumental acts (both questions and answers) to social-emotional acts (both positive and negative reactions). The average ratio for normal groups is around two instrumental acts to each social-emotional act. Where the ratio is higher than two to one it may mean that the group members are highly task oriented, are confronted with a job to do, possess consensus with respect to their work, and feel a necessity to accomplish the job quickly and efficiently. However, a ratio higher than two to one may also mean that the

[7] Hugh Philp and Dexter Dunphy, "Developmental Trends in Small Groups," *Sociometry,* 22, 1959, pp. 162-174.

group's members are anxious about their relations to each other, are convinced that social-emotional acts are inappropriate in the situation, or are behaving in ways which inhibit the expression of social-emotional acts.

On the other hand, a ratio of instrumental to social-emotional acts that is less than two to one may mean that the group's members are primarily concerned with developing a sense of solidarity or cohesion by seeking to resolve interpersonal conflicts among members or to demonstrate feelings of warmth and cohesion. However, a ratio of less than two to one may also mean that the group's members are avoiding their work. Variation in the ratio of instrumental to social-emotional acts is partly a function of the established norms of a group, partly a function of the personal inclinations of group members, and partly a function of the nature of the group itself (that is, its objectives, the situation it is confronted with, and similar factors). The ratio tends to be high in groups where established norms reward instrumental acts and punish social-emotional acts, high in groups where the members pride themselves in being rational and in suppressing or inhibiting their feelings, and high in problem-solving business conferences. Instrumental and social-emotional acts are interdependent: too great a ratio of either one or the other leads to a counterreaction so that over time in most groups the ratio approaches a balance of two to one.

Comparisons of satisfied and dissatisfied groups and analyses of profiles of all groups may serve as a basis for depicting the kind of balance among types of communicative acts which characterize problem-solving groups and as a criterion for locating trouble. First, it is important to note that some time must be devoted to the expression of questions and feelings. If the percentage of answers rises too high, the group action may be perceived as a "dictated decision." If the percentage of answers is too low, it may be seen as "a waste of time."

Second, there is typically a balance of about two positive reactions to each negative reaction. If the percentage of negative reactions is too high, the group meeting seems to become a name-calling session, with a build-up of disagreement to an explosive point. Or, if the percentage of negative reactions is too low, the meeting becomes a mutual admiration society in which disagreements are repressed, inhibited, or absent by reason of lack of involvement.

Analysis of the distribution of acts over time suggests that the typical group emphasizes problems of orientation (facts and information) in the early phase of a meeting, problems of evaluation (opinions) in the middle phase, and problems of control and decision (suggestions) in the end phase. Concomitant with these three phases, there seems to be an increase in both positive and negative reactions, with some indication that though negative reactions tend to increase, after a group reaches agreement a final expression of positive reactions seems to ensue.

Some common types of participation in groups may be depicted (or established) through analyses of the distribution of members' acts. Data gathered from the members through questionnaires also furnish a basis for depicting such types. Communicative activity is one aspect of participation; the more satisfied groups tend to exhibit a fairly clear differentiation from the most communicatively active member to the least active. Group functioning is affected by the proportion and kind of participators: those groups whose members get involved in competition for the floor and who do not listen to each other are found to have all or mostly high participators; groups deficient in activity are found to have all or mostly low participators.

Among the highest participators there tends to be a differentiation between the person who emphasizes answers, whose acts are dominantly ideas, facts, suggestions, and the like, and the person who, though fairly active with respect to answers, is also quite reactive. The former is referred to as the task leader, the latter as the social-emotional leader. The task leader's contribution to the group is to influence and control the solutions to the problems of orientation, evaluation, and control; the social-emotional leader's contribution is to influence and control the solutions to the problems of decision, tension management, and integration. Though the task and social-emotional leaders differ somewhat in the nature of their activity, they complement each other and, in a satisfied group, they support each other.

Other typical roles are not so clear-cut except for the role of member. One may speculate that the dominant, "loud-mouth" person might be high on activity which seems often to be ir- relevant to the flow of communication, and that the "scapegoat" might be exceedingly low on activity. In addition, the typical balance of types of acts might suggest that a group with a clearly differentiated leadership, with task and social-emotional leaders supporting each other, and with differentiation in participation of members, could not only absorb one or two difficult members but might in fact need such members to maintain an effective balance among types of acts. For example, shy members who disagree might express their disagreement if they were stimu- lated by a person who seems always to disagree, or, if they agree, might express that agreement as a reaction to the same person.

The analysis of the communicative behavior of members of small groups on the basis of the category scheme is not ex- hausted by the comments above. Bales has analyzed rather ex- tensively the sequence of proaction (succeeding act by the same person) and reaction (succeeding act by another person), the problem of shifting leadership when a popular member (a social- emotional leader) who is also an active member (a task leader) confronts the dilemma that he cannot be both (except in rare cases), and the like. But the discussion above provides a basic outline of IPA that gives an indication of the usefulness of the scheme and of its ability to generate a host of interpretations and descriptions of the behavior of members of small groups.

Bales's system also involves a theory about small groups, as was indicated in the first few paragraphs of this section. Briefly put, Bales's theory postulates a group which, as members com- municate with each other, solves the basic problems which con- front it in such a way that members are able to achieve their tasks and to build solidarity. Bales further theorizes that task achievement and the development of solidarity tend to be opposed, so that the total state of the problem solutions tends to be a dynamic equilibrium in which the group swings, like a pendulum, from an emphasis on task achievement to an emphasis on building solidarity, back and forth as circumstances warrant.

Thus, where Lewin's field theory seems to be most useful as a perspective with which to approach the analysis of a group, Bales's IPA seems to be most useful as a scheme for the analysis of the behavior of members of a group. And, to anticipate the next section, Homans's system theory seems to be most useful as a device to synthesize the findings of studies of small groups.

HOMANS'S SYSTEM THEORY

Homans's system theory is most clearly developed in his book *The Human Group*,[8] where the basic concepts and propositions are outlined. Since that publication his theory has been subjected to various analyses and criticisms. He has modified it in two major publications, first in a chapter in *The Handbook of Social Psychology*,[9] and most recently in a second book, *Social Behavior: Its Elementary Forms*.[10] The analysis presented here is based primarily on his first publication, with minor modifications drawn from the later ones.

Homans's theory is developed on the basis of a major assumption which differentiates his theory from that of Bales or Lewin. Where Lewin was concerned with developing an abstract set of concepts to apply to the forces present in an individual's or group's situation, and where Bales was primarily concerned with developing a scheme for classifying communicative acts, Homans is concerned with developing a set of concepts that are close to everyday life. Homans's basic position is best presented in his words:[11]

[8] George C. Homans, *The Human Group* (New York: Harcourt, 1950).
[9] Henry W. Riecken and George C. Homans, "Psychological Aspects of Social Structure," in Gardner Lindzey (ed.), *Handbook of Social Psychology, Volume II* (Cambridge, Mass.: Addison-Wesley, 1954), pp. 786-832.
[10] George C. Homans, *Social Behavior: Its Elementary Forms* (New York: Harcourt, 1961).
[11] *The Human Group, op. cit.* in note 8, p. 5.

"But in sociology we have not made as much progress as we might have, and the reason is clear. We have pursued the higher branches of our science before the trunk was strong. We have not grown because we have had nothing to grow from. We have given ink-blot tests to Navahos; we have computed differential fertility rates among ethnic groups in Kansas—all worthy subjects if we had also studied ordinary, everyday social behavior. Make no mistake about it, *that* we have not done. . . . Far from discovering facts that are too familiar, we have not discovered facts that are familiar enough."

Homans argues that his theory and his concepts will be as close to observable events as he can make them and, by making them so, he hopes that he will help direct the attention of others to the analysis of the familiar and commonplace. In this way, Homans feels, two things will be accomplished: first, his theory will avoid an ivory-tower death, and, second, his interpretations will be consistent with everyday life, since they will emerge from analysis of concrete behavior. Not that Homans advocates "the attitude of daily life"—rather, he advocates a close articulation between his concepts and events observable in daily life.

Homans's theory consists essentially of two parts: part one includes three concepts and relations among these concepts which form the elementary aspects of social behavior, and part two includes more abstract concepts and relations among these concepts which are, in part, defined in terms of the elementary concepts.

First, let us consider the three elementary concepts. Homans argues that when an individual seeks to describe the behavior of people in everyday life, sticking closely to their actual behavior and avoiding imputing motivations or meanings to them insofar as possible, the description will likely include three types of comments. First, statements of *activities*, referring to movements, action, work, typing, milking, writing, driving a car, and the like. These are, basically, things people do to or with nonhuman objects, or with other people when their reaction or reciprocal be-

havior is ignored (such as cutting a person's hair). Second, statements of *sentiments,* referring to feelings (happy, sad, angry,
stern, loving), to attitudes (this is his job, it is time to go, he is
conservative), or to beliefs. These constitute the inner state of
the person, the things an individual subjectively perceives. And,
third, statements about *interaction,* including going with someone, going to see someone, eating together, playing together,
working together, and the like. The basic characteristic of interaction is that it is behavior directed toward another person when
his reaction or reciprocal behavior is taken into account.

Activity, interaction, and sentiment are the elementary forms
of behavior, the three basic concepts of Homans's theory. These
are related to each other in the form of three basic hypotheses:
(1) "both motives and associated activities persist, both con-
tinuously recreated, but if either side of the relationship is
changed, the other will be affected;"[12] (2) "if the scheme of activities is changed, the scheme of interaction will, in general,
change also, and vice versa;"[13] and (3) "interaction and positive
sentiments (friendliness) are directly related."[14]

These three basic hypotheses are modified and elaborated in
various ways, but they can serve here as illustrative of the style
of Homans's analysis although there are probably a hundred or
more hypotheses in *The Human Group,* and it is impractical to
include all of them here. The basic point Homans is seeking to
make in this analysis is that interaction, sentiment, and activity
are dynamically related so that a change in one will lead to a
change in the others. Thus the behavior of members of a group
must be considered as a system of behavior, and not as discrete
behaviors unrelated to each other.

The system which emerges is developed in part two of Homans's theory. Basically, Homans conceives a social system as
the character and state of relations among interaction, activity,
and sentiment among a collection of two or more persons who

---

[12] *Ibid.,* p. 99.
[13] *Ibid.,* p. 102.
[14] *Ibid.;* see discussion pp. 61 ff. of this book.

are identifiable as a unity (a work group, a family, a clique). This social system is constituted of two parts: *an external system,* the relations among interaction, activity, and sentiment which are imposed on a group by forces external to it (such as a larger group, a manager, a national office, the local police force); and an *internal system,* the relations among interaction, activity, and sentiment which are spontaneously elaborated and standardized by members of the group.

Any social system, then, consists of an external and an internal component, though their relative dominance may vary. The external system among the members of a street-corner gang is relatively vague, consisting mostly of legal restrictions and other constraints or expectations applicable to people in general. On the other hand, the external system of a work group is relatively explicit, defining a man's activities in his job, the interactions he is expected to have with his coworkers or his boss, and some of the sentiments he is expected to have (such as a motivation to work hard, value pay, and be satisfied). This difference in the relative dominance of the external and internal systems leads Homans to develop the concept of *autonomy,* referring to the degree to which the members of a group are free to develop an internal system. A group with high autonomy would be likely to have a vague external system, a group with low autonomy a specific external system. In the former case, an internal system must develop quite elaborately if there is to be a social system in operation at all. In the latter case, an internal system may be only weakly developed but the group may still function effectively since the external system is explicit.

For any group the external system is a given—it probably existed before the group began, and it may well continue to exist even if the group should disband. However, Homans does develop a hypothesis in which he argues that the internal system can serve as the source for changes in the external system, and vice versa. But of more interest here is that any group is apt to develop at least a rudimentary internal system, and in the process of development three modes may be discerned: elaboration, differentiation, and standardization. The mode of *elaboration* refers to the process whereby individuals embellish their activities in ways over and beyond that required of them in the external system, just as their sentiments are not restricted to those expected of them, nor their interactions only what the external system decrees. A private may be required to salute an officer, but the private does not have to smile when he salutes. Or, if the private does smile, this smile may in fact mask unpleasant feelings. Sentiments, of course, are notoriously difficult to detect accurately, and even more difficult to change or control. Activities and interactions may be more amenable to control by others, but even here various subtle aspects may be as difficult to control as sentiments. Consequently, few people stick closely to the activity, interaction, and sentiment required by them in the external system of a group, and the particular style of embellishment becomes a part of the mode of elaboration.

As the members of a group express their personal styles of behavior which go beyond the requirements of the external system, these behaviors become differentiated and the members of a group begin to recognize them and to attach varying degrees of value to them. Some activities, sentiments, and interactions begin to be highly valued, others less valued, some ignored, and others negatively valued. The mode of *differentiation* refers to the process of recognition and evaluation of differences. As the internal system is spontaneously elaborated and differentiated, variations in value and habit lead to the routinization of certain activities, interactions, and sentiments, a process which Homans calls the mode of *standardization.*

The modes of elaboration, differentiation, and standardization refer to the phases through which the internal system of a group evolves. This internal system becomes the second component of the group's social system, evolving spontaneously as a product of the unique qualities of the members of a group, but once evolved, becoming routinized and affecting not only the social system of the group as a whole, but its external system as well.

As Homans develops the concept of the social system of a

group it becomes necessary to introduce more concepts to refer to observed characteristics of the social system. Members of a group are usually differentiated in terms of *rank,* a concept referring to a man's position in the group relative to other members. Rank may be accorded both in the external system and in the internal system. The group also has a set of expectations regarding the behavior of members, *norms* which regulate the expected interactions, activities, and sentiments of members both in the external and in the internal system. Finally, *role* refers to the characteristic pattern of a member's activities, interactions, and sentiments, along with his rank and the degree to which he conforms to the norms.

Along with the introduction of this second set of concepts, Homans also presents a number of hypotheses expressing the relations among these concepts. Some illustrative hypotheses are: (1) the higher a man's rank in a group, the more closely he conforms to the norms of a group; (2) the higher a man's rank in a group, the more leeway he has in conforming to the norms (the more likely nonconformity will be overlooked or will be interpreted as in the interests of the group, rather than as a threat to the group); (3) the higher a man's rank in a group, the more interaction he will have as a group representative with nongroup members; (4) pressure is exerted on members of a group to maintain their established degree of conformity to the norms (and not to increase their conformity, since this might upset the rank hierarchy).

So much for the basic elements of Homans's theory. Various other hypotheses and concepts are developed as Homans applies his scheme to more complex groups and to group relations. Homans's system theory has a remarkable ability to synthesize a host of observations and empirical findings, and is richly productive of hypotheses.

OTHER THEORIES

The field of small groups has given rise to many other theories. The three discussed above constitute the most popular, but their

popularity will likely be attenuated as succeeding writers introduce major modifications or largely new theories which seem to
fit the data somewhat better or offer a more comprehensive
sweep. Homans has extended his theory in a 1961 publication[15]
by linking it to behavioral psychology and elementary economics, introducing a few general propositions about reward,
cost, satiation, investment, profit, and value, from which (Homans
argues) the propositions discussed above can be derived. Thibaut
and Kelley[16] have extended field theory in a similar direction, by
focusing on role and one's role repertoire and developing a series
of propositions involving rewards and costs which describe some
of the conditions under which a given behavior is enacted.

Hemphill[17] and Cattell[18] have sought to develop descriptive
schemes of group characteristics, and have used a factor analytic
procedure as a device to reduce a large number of characteristics
to a few major factors. Borgatta and Cottrell[19] have used a similar procedure and have, with Meyer,[20] discussed some of the
problems and some of the potentialities of factor analytic procedures. It seems reasonable to assume that factor analysis and
other quantitative procedures will help clarify empirical findings
and their linkage to theories, though to date these procedures
do not seem to add very much clarification or advantage to the
three general theories discussed above.

Goffman[21] has described some of the strategies people use to
present themselves to others so as to maintain an intended ap-

[15] *Social Behavior, op. cit.* in note 10.

[16] John W. Thibaut and Harold H. Kelley, *The Social Psychology of
Groups* (New York: Wiley, 1959).

[17] John K. Hemphill, *Group Dimensions: A Manual for Their Measure-
ment* (Ohio State University Bureau of Business Research Monograph, No.
87, 1950).

[18] R. B. Cattell, "New Concepts for Measuring Leadership, in Terms of
Group Syntality," *Human Relations*, 4, 1951, pp. 161-184.

[19] E. F. Borgatta and L. S. Cottrell, Jr., "On the Classification of Groups,"
Sociometry, 18, 1955, pp. 665-678.

[20] E. F. Borgatta, L. S. Cottrell, Jr., and H. J. Meyer, "On the Dimensions of Group Behavior," *Sociometry*, 19, 1956, pp. 223-240.

[21] Erving Goffman, *The Presentation of Self in Everyday Life* (New
York: Doubleday, 1959).

pearance, or to "unmask" another or to penetrate his "front." Goffman converts Shakespeare's "all the world's a stage" into a serious attempt to develop concepts about behavior. Thus a small group engages in two major types of behavior: *up-stage*, the presentation of a "front," the behavior of members of a group when in the presence of outsiders, especially an audience of customers, clients, bosses, and the like; and *back-stage*, the development and maintenance of a front, the behavior of members in a group when not in the presence of outsiders. Goffman's contribution lies not only in his ingenious use of stage talk, but also in his specification of strategies, the conditions under which they are employed, and the role of physical objects (props).

Theoretical writing about small groups has progressed in several different directions, as the illustrations above indicate. Two of the most promising directions are the tieing of a general theory of small groups to a more fundamental or basic theory (the work of Homans and of Thibaut and Kelley), and the development of a middle range (limited) theory designed to structure findings dealing with some aspect of small groups (the work of Festinger, of Kelman, of Blau, and of Bennis and Shepard).

HOMANS

Homans's tieing of his general system theory to a set of principles drawn from behavioral psychology and elementary economics is provocative and intriguing. The hypotheses and propositions developed in his *The Human Group* are organized around the concepts of activity, interaction, and sentiment, and are derived from or illustrated by a few studies of groups in a natural setting: a street-corner gang, a work group in a factory, a family in a preliterate society. In *Social Behavior*, his later book, he directs his attention to two things not discussed earlier: motivation and laboratory research.

As to motivation—why does an individual engage in some activity, interact with another person, or hold certain sentiments?— the answers, Homans argues, must be drawn from behavioral psychology and elementary economics. From these two disciplines Homans derives a number of basic propositions which he feels provide the motivational underpinning necessary to round out one side of the theory presented earlier. In the statement of these propositions Homans uses the term *activity* to refer to behavior expressed or emitted by a person, a usage which makes it broader in meaning than the term *activity* in *The Human Group.*

Some of these basic propositions about motivation are found in Chapter 4 of *Social Behavior: Its Elementary Forms,* and may be summarized as follows:

1. *Activity is directly related to the similarity of a stimulus-situation to a past stimulus-situation in which activity was rewarded.* With this proposition Homans argues that the motive underlying a given activity is that the person has found the activity rewarding in the past. In any given situation a person is motivated to express those activities which he has found in the past to be rewarding, and to suppress those activities which he has found in the past not to be rewarding, to be punished, or perhaps to be ignored.

2. *Activity and reward are directly related.* This proposition implies that when a person has a choice among two or more activities which have been rewarding in the past he will elect to express that one which has been most rewarding.

3. *The relation between activity and reward is enhanced by the presence of value, and reduced by the presence of satiation.* With this proposition the relation between activity and reward is elaborated. Value (a *sentiment* in Homans's earlier conceptual scheme) enhances the likelihood of an activity being expressed, so that of two activities equally rewarding on grounds other than value the one considered more valuable will be expressed. Satiation (the continued expression of an activity to the point where it ceases to be rewarding) reduces the relation, in that of two activities equally rewarding, the one which has been expressed most recently, if it has led to satiation, will be suppressed and the alternative activity will be expressed.

4. *Activity and cost are inversely related.* When a person has

a choice among two or more activities which have been costly in the past (*cost* is to be used as the opposite of *reward*), he will likely elect to express that one which has been least costly.

5. *The relation between activity and cost is reduced by value, and enhanced by satiation.* If an activity is costly but valuable a person may express it and bear the cost; but if a person is satiated an activity may not be expressed even though only mildly costly.

6. *The presence of alternative activities is increased sharply by the introduction of a third person into a two-person situation, such that satiation becomes much less likely to occur or to affect activity.* In a two-person situation Homans argues that the first five propositions go far toward explaining why certain activities are expressed or suppressed and why the propositions hold which are induced from an analysis of the case studies as presented in *The Human Group.* However, when a third person is introduced into the situation, Homans argues that satiation becomes much less operative because so many alternative activities become available. This proposition underscores the idea that as groups increase in size beyond two their relationships become exceedingly complex.

7. *Distributive justice and emotionality are inversely related, such that where a person's costs are high in his activities, he should be rewarded, and where a person has a great deal invested in something, he should be rewarded.* In this proposition Homans argues that when a person has invested a lot of time and energy in some activity there is a strong feeling that he should be rewarded to some degree for this fact alone (seniority, for example: letting a senior play football even though he may not be as good as a sophomore), and also that a person deserves some reward if his costs are high (persons who endanger their lives in pursuit of their job, such as miners, demolition experts, or spies). This proposition is derived more from elementary economics, whereas the first six propositions are derived somewhat more from behavioral psychology.

The second thing not discussed in *The Human Group* is laboratory research. In *Social Behavior*, Homans seeks to elaborate in more precise ways various propositions about human behavior drawn from the extensive research literature. For each study presented Homans does two things: first, he summarizes the research study and its findings, and, second, he discusses the relation of these findings to the propositions outlined in *The Human Group* and to those outlined above in *Social Behavior*.

THIBAUT AND KELLEY

Thibaut and Kelley have done a similar job in *The Social Psychology of Groups*, where they have drawn on behavioral psychology and on elementary economics for their propositions about behavior. It is, perhaps, an indication of the developing maturity of the theory of small groups (and of social psychology in general) that they also stress the concepts of reward, cost, value, satiation, justice, and others emphasized by Homans, and seek to develop a basic proposition that when two (or more) people interact, each elects to express a behavior which will provide him with the greatest reward and the least cost. Thibaut and Kelley stress the point that almost any behavior is both rewarding and costly, and that the decision to express a given behavior is based on the balance of reward and cost for that behavior in comparison with the reward-cost balance of a potential alternative behavior.

There are some limitations on the usefulness of economic models of interpersonal behavior. A major limitation is that they assume that man is essentially a rational animal, capable of accurately taking into account the rewards and costs of some potential behavior and capable of enacting the most rewarding or avoiding the most costly behavior. Thibaut and Kelley, and Homans, discuss various limitations on their models and conclude that the limitations are not insurmountable but can be overcome partly by taking more things into account in assessing what a person considers rewarding or costly. As more things are taken into account, however, the model becomes less of an economic model. There is no doubt that the use of an economic model (or of Homans's behavioral-psychology model) provides the basis for logical rigor, but there is also no doubt that much social behavior is inconsistent with predictions from the model.

The development of middle-range theories proceeds in a different direction though with a similar method. These theories take some aspect of small-group behavior and seek to develop a set of basic propositions which will summarize the findings relevant to a given area and provide a basis for deriving testable hypotheses. Several of these theories will be discussed briefly below.

FESTINGER

Festinger (a student of Lewin's) has developed two middle-range theories: a theory of social-comparison processes[22] and a theory of cognitive dissonance.[23] In the theory of social-comparison processes Festinger states, in a few propositions, some of the factors underlying the process of influence on opinions held by members of a small group. Briefly, he contends that people are motivated to evaluate their opinions and abilities, and that for opinions, and often for abilities, the only source of evaluation is in the reactions of others and not in some objective standard. (When an objective standard is available, Festinger argues that people will usually utilize it.) Furthermore, he holds that people will compare themselves with others who are fairly similar to them, and not with others who are quite different. Festinger develops various other propositions to express aspects of the process of comparison and its effects on opinions and abilities, particularly the pressures toward uniformity.

In the theory of cognitive dissonance, Festinger seeks to develop a theory to explain why a person holds a given opinion or expresses a given behavior, or changes his opinion or modifies his behavior. Briefly, he argues that there exists in the human be-

---

[22] Leon Festinger, "A Theory of Social Comparison Processes," *Human Relations*, 7, 1954, pp. 117-140.

[23] Leon Festinger, *A Theory of Cognitive Dissonance* (Evanston, Ill.: Row, Peterson, 1957).

ing a drive to maintain a general sense of consonance of one's opinions, ideas, attitudes, and the like, a sense of their being consistent with each other, of going together in a meaningful way. When some aspects of a person's mental life seem awry, seem to be dissonant with other aspects, there is a drive (the person is motivated) to reduce the dissonance. The reduction of dissonance may be accomplished in many different ways: a person may ignore some things, he may reinterpret observations he has made, or he may modify other attitudes or opinions in order to reduce dissonance. Man may be a dissonance-reducing organism, but this does not necessarily mean that man is a dissonance-avoiding organism. Some experimental evidence suggests that man does not avoid dissonance and may, in fact, seek it out.

KELMAN

Kelman has developed a theory of social influence[24] in which he distinguishes three processes of influence operative in social situations.

Compliance is a process in which a person adopts an attitude or opinion another person or group wants him to adopt in order to obtain a favorable reaction from the other person or group, without actually accepting or believing in the attitude or opinion. An example would be a subordinate's expressing agreement with his supervisor in order to curry favor with the latter, but privately and inwardly disagreeing. This process is operative when an individual wishes to insure that other people in the situation think favorably of him, and when the other people are in a position to reward him in some fashion. Some of the consequences of compliance are that the compliant individual is likely to express or hold the attitude or opinion only when in the company of others, and that his expression of attitude may change as he moves from one situation to another or as the perception

[24] Herbert C. Kelman, "Processes of Opinion Change," *Public Opinion Quarterly*, 25, 1961, pp. 57-78; see also Warren G. Bennis, "A Case Study in Research Formulation," *International Journal of Group Psychotherapy*, 11, 1961, pp. 272-283.

of other people as capable of rewarding him changes. For example, an athlete may disagree with a stranger concerning football strategy, but if he finds out that the stranger is the coach of a football team to which the athlete aspires he may change his attitudes to agree with the stranger's attitudes.

Identification is a process of influence in which an individual adopts an attitude or opinion of another person or group because he identifies with the person or group, takes over the person's role, and incorporates the other person or group in his own self-image. An example would be the kind of influence a father exerts over his son, in which the son seeks to be like his father because it is self-satisfying to be so. Another example would be the kind of influence exerted by a powerful figure over his followers when the followers become disciples or converts. In these cases the individual being influenced is concerned with his self concept and sense of identity, and finds that a powerful figure provides a model of what he wishes to become. A consequence of this type of influence is that the individual is most likely to continue to hold the attitudes and opinions which he has taken over from someone else only as long as the other person has an important relationship to him and provides him with a sense of identity, self-esteem, and self-satisfaction (for example, Germans who once adored Adolf Hitler may now be repulsed by him).

Internalization occurs when a person adopts an attitude as his own because it is consistent with his perspective, because it solves a problem for him. In this case an individual is confronted with a problem or with a sense of uncertainty or ambiguity concerning something he is interested in. Another person or group offers a solution or a suggestion and, because the tendered idea seems credible, he adopts it. An example of internalization would be the "ah ha" phenomenon, the discovery of a solution to some problem with which a person may have been struggling for some time. In this case the source of the solution is of minor importance, and the person is not motivated to accept the solution because others will like him if he does so (as in compliance) or because he wishes to be like a respected or revered person

(as in identification). One consequence of internalization is that
the influence exerted comes to be more lasting because the individual incorporates it into his own value system, into his perspective and his style of behavior.

These three processes of influence may be said to function in
somewhat different contexts and ways. Compliance may be the
major kind of influence which peers exert on each other, as in
the world of teen-age fads and fashions or in the phenomenon of
delinquent acts by teen-agers who later become model law-abid-
ing adults. Identification may be the major kind of influence
which authority figures exert over others, as in the cases of parents' influence on children, teachers' influence on students, or
master craftsmen's influence on apprentices. Internalization may
be the major kind of influence which psychiatrists exert on pa-
tients (if the therapy is successful), or which some teachers exert
on students when the teachers seek to develop the students'
problem-solving abilities in the spirit of John Dewey's prag-
matic philosophy.

BLAU

Blau has presented a theory of social integration[25] in which he
seeks to explain why and how persons become accepted as members of groups. His basic argument is that the newcomer seeks
acceptance on two grounds: first, he attempts to impress others
with his good qualities, with his attractiveness to them so that
they will wish to accept him as a group member. However, Blau
argues, the more impressive a newcomer appears the more re-
luctant group members become to accept him. His attractiveness
constitutes a potential threat to the established relations and
hierarchy among the members, so that they may become defensive and suspicious. The result is that the newcomer, in his
desire to impress group members with his attractiveness, may
also appear to be unapproachable. Consequently the newcomer

[25] Peter M. Blau, "A Theory of Social Integration," *American Journal of
Sociology*, 65, 1960, pp. 545-556.

must somehow present himself as approachable, as someone who, though attractive to others, is also modest and, perhaps, even foolish at times. This "self-deprecating modesty" helps members become less defensive and less suspicious, and more ready to accept the newcomer in the group.

Blau argues that success in becoming accepted in a group involves both attractiveness and approachability, and that a newcomer is most likely to be successful if he first attempts to impress others with his good qualities and then demonstrates his approachability with well-chosen self-deprecating modesty. His weaknesses are important, for if he unwittingly demonstrates weakness in things highly valued by the group, he may, on balance, be perceived as unattractive. The processes of attractiveness and approachability lead to social integration and, at the same time, to social differentiation, for a person's valued qualities are not only attractive but also cause others to develop feelings of respect toward him and a desire to reward him in some way. The deference and differential rewards accruing to valued members of a group lead to feelings of unapproachability, however, so that members are, because of differentiation, led to counteract divisive effects by demonstrating their approachability, their "humanness" and proneness to errors and mistakes. Thus social differentiation, in turn, leads to social integration. Acceptance in a group, in Blau's theory, depends on both attractiveness and approachability.

EMOTIONALITY THEORIES

Bion[26] has focused on still another aspect of group behavior, the emotional factor. In the theories discussed above, emotionality has not been excluded but has been more or less embodied as a part of the total analysis. In Lewin's scheme, emotion enters primarily as a residual factor which helps explain why people are

[26] W. R. Bion, "Experiences in Groups," *Human Relations,* 1, 1948, pp. 314-320 and 487-496; 2, 1949, pp. 13-22 and 295-303; 3, 1950, pp. 3-14 and 395-402; 4, 1951, pp. 221-227; ——, "Group Dynamics: A Review," *International Journal of Psychoanalysis,* 33, 1952, pp. 235-247.

motivated to achieve goals, to overcome barriers, to perceive or fail to perceive objects in their environment. In Bales's category scheme, emotion is embodied explicitly in six categories, but since acts which are classified under positive and negative reactions are mostly statements expressed by members, emotions are not expressly distinguished from ideas. The same is true for Homans's concepts, in which emotion is included under the broad element of sentiment but what is discussed and observed constitutes expressed opinions, attitudes, and values.

Emotion is an elusive aspect of human behavior. It is difficult to describe, to express, and often even to recognize. It is usually located in the physiology of the body, but it has learned qualities. People can vividly experience emotion and yet find their tongues silent when they seek to describe it to others. Instruments may be used to record changes in pulse, temperature, perspiration, and muscle tone, but the meaning of such records remains confusing. It is understandable that few theorists, though recognizing its importance, would attempt to describe and analyze emotion and include it as a major category.

Bion, being a psychotherapist, is not averse to focusing on emotionality and he is willing to ignore the thinking processes and to develop a theory dealing exclusively with emotionality. He does not deny the importance of task activity, but argues that work and emotionality are two sides to group behavior and he is willing to let others focus on work. Thus his theory should be treated as a partial theory of small groups, a theory dealing only with emotionality that must be supplemented by a theory of work to round out the picture.

In his theory Bion argues that there are four major emotions experienced in groups: fight, flight, pairing, and dependency. At any point in the life of a group one of these emotions is dominant—the group may be in a fighting mood, for example, and almost every comment, no matter how innocuous, seems to call for a hostile reply; or it may be in a flight mood and unable to deal with any issue, evading or ignoring things with which it should deal; or it may be in a pairing mood, in which one or more pairs of members are carrying on personal conversations with the unspoken approval of the others; or it may be in a dependent mood, in which the group, rather than tackle its problem, tries to get someone or something to solve it. Bion develops a theory about the sources of these moods and about their effects, including conceptions of the typical sequence of moods a group goes through. Other theories about emotionality tend to focus on only two emotions, intimacy and control. In these theories Bion's concepts of fight, flight, and dependency are included in the concept of control, and pairing in intimacy. Bennis and Shepard[27] have built up a theory of group development which emphasizes the process through which members of a group struggle with two major questions: How close are they to get to each other? Who is to control the group? Much of what happens in the first few meetings of a group is seen to revolve around these two issues. Thus some members may desire to maintain a certain aloofness toward others, whereas other members may seek close, personal ties. On the other hand, some members may seek to find someone they can be dependent on, a chairman who will be a strong paternal leader, whereas other members may resist allowing anyone else to control them, seeking instead to maintain independence. But if a group has work to do it must resolve the intimacy and control problems. It cannot spend all its energy arguing about how intimate members are to get with each other, nor about who is to exert how much control. Members cannot be too aloof lest they become or remain indifferent to the group's work, but neither can they become too intimate lest they decide their friendship is more important than their work. Similarly, they cannot become dependent on one or a few persons lest they lose a great deal of their potential, nor can they function very well as so many individuals each safeguarding his autonomy.

The resolution of these problems is held to be largely a func-

[27] Warren G. Bennis and Herbert A. Shepard, "A Theory of Group Development," *Human Relations*, 9, 1956, pp. 415-457; William C. Schutz, *FIRO: A Three-Dimensional Theory of Interpersonal Behavior* (New York: Rinehart, 1958); ——, "Interpersonal Underworld," *Harvard Business Review*, 36, July-August 1958, pp. 123-135.

tion of time and the degree of awareness that they exist. If subgroups form and battle lines are drawn some resolution is likely to occur. The resolution may be disbanding or some form of compromise, and the problem may be resurrected later—indeed, it probably will be if the group exists for any length of time. Several writers have developed theories about the existence, development of awareness, and types of resolutions of the intimacy and control problems. It is sufficient to note that these problems are considered the core of the emotional life of a group, affecting, and in turn being affected by, the work or task activities of a group. Adherents of the emotionality theory of group life argue that when people disagree with each other they may be either disagreeing with what each other said or expressing disagreement with each other's unstated position about intimacy or control. And they may be aware or unaware of the reason for their disagreement.

CONCLUSION

The art of speculation about small groups is well developed. Although there are not one or two widely accepted and validated theories about small groups, there are at least three theories widely utilized, either in their original or in a modified form. There are also several (almost numerous) other theories, some declaring their affinity to Lewin or Bales or Homans, others to Sullivan[28] or Freud,[29] and still others to various sources. For the armchair theorizer the field of small groups is enticing.

The field is also attractive to the researcher, whether in the laboratory or in the field, whether quantitatively or qualitatively oriented, whether interested in the details of behavior or in testing theories. This blend of theoretical and empirical attractiveness promises to be fruitful for the development of "hardheaded" scientific knowledge.

But which theory is best? Which theory is most logical, encom-

[28] Harry Stack Sullivan, *The Interpersonal Theory of Psychiatry* (New York: Norton, 1954).
[29] Sigmund Freud, *Group Psychology and the Analysis of the Ego* (New York: Liveright, 1949; 1st ed., London: Hogarth, 1922).

passes the greatest amount of research findings, predicts most widely? These questions cannot be answered unequivocally, for the answer depends on what kinds of assumptions a person makes, what kinds of things he wishes to predict, what uses he wants to make of the theory. For the beginning student, it is probably wise to choose either Lewin, Bales, or Homans, learn this theory thoroughly, then take up the others that interest him. It is wise not because they are necessarily the best, but because an understanding of one of them will enable an individual to read more widely in the field, since a large proportion of the literature will make at least passing reference to them or be fairly easily translatable into their language.

Finally, the art of speculation, to the scientist, is not sacred. A theory is a guide—it sensitizes an individual to certain things and encourages him to ignore other things. A theory is also predictive and explanatory—it must serve as a source of hypotheses to be tested and it must be able to integrate research findings. A careful comparison of theories on these criteria might produce an unequivocal ranking of "goodness" but even this is currently in doubt. It is surprising to see how flexible the various theories are, how additions and modifications can be introduced to account for findings or to lead to new hypotheses. In the final analysis a scientific theory is as good as its explanatory and predictive ability. If a field theorist, a system theorist, and an emotionality theorist can talk sense to each other, that capacity may be as much as can be presently asked for.

Selected Bibliography for Chapter 3

Aside from the references listed in the footnotes of this chapter, the student should consult the following books.

GENERAL

Michael Argyle, *The Scientific Study of Social Behavior* (New York: Philosophical Library, 1957), especially Chapters 4 and 5. Argyle presents a survey of theory and research on interaction and small groups and includes references to British researchers not usually found in American books.

Robert T. Golombiewski, *The Small Group: An Analysis of Research Concepts and Operations* (Chicago: University of Chicago Press, 1962). A discussion with particular attention to logical analysis and to the problems of generalizing from the results of a specific study.

Josephine Klein, *The Study of Groups* (London: Routledge, 1956). A survey of research findings of both American and British investigators, organized around a small number of assumptions (or propositions).

Michael S. Olmsted, *The Small Group* (New York: Random House, 1959). An introduction to the study of small groups, including a summary of early field studies, a survey of research findings, and a brief discussion of selected theories.

FIELD THEORY

Dorwin Cartwright and Alvin Zander (eds.), *Group Dynamics* (2d ed.; Evanston, Ill.: Row, Peterson, 1960). Cartwright and Zander were students or colleagues of Kurt Lewin, and their formulations of small-group theory contained in Chapters 1, 7, 11, 22, 28, and 36 of the first edition and Chapters 1, 2, 3, 9, 19, 25, and 34 of the second edition are in Lewin's tradition. The selection of readings included in both editions also reflects some of the best research by investigators using the field theoretical perspective, as well as other perspectives.

Morton Deutsch, "Field Theory in Social Psychology," in Gardner Lindzey, *Handbook of Social Psychology, Volume I* (Cambridge, Mass.: Addison-Wesley, 1954), pp. 181-222. Deutsch's discussion of field theory is generally considered to be the best-reasoned analysis in the literature.

Kurt Lewin (Dorwin Cartwright, ed.), *Field Theory in Social Science* (New York: Harper, 1951), especially Chapters VI, VII, IX, and X. This book contains most of the theoretical papers of Lewin.

Kurt Lewin (Gertrud Weiss Lewin, ed.), *Resolving Social Conflicts* (New York: Harper, 1948), especially Part II. This book contains a summary of much of the research which Lewin conducted or guided and provides a discussion of his perspective on various social problems (applied social psychology).

R. W. Leeper, *Lewin's Topological and Vector Psychology: A Digest and a Critique* (Eugene, Ore.: University of Oregon Press, 1943). Leeper's analysis is considered the classic treatment of Lewin's work and of field theory.

SYSTEM THEORY

Robert F. Bales, *Interaction Process Analysis* (Cambridge, Mass.: Addison-Wesley, 1950); Talcott Parsons, Robert F. Bales, and Edward A. Shils, *Working Papers in the Theory of Action* (Glencoe, Ill.: Free Press, 1953). These two books provide a discussion of Bales's theory and its relation to broader sociological theory, as well as summaries of the early research using Bales's category scheme.

George C. Homans, *The Human Group* (New York: Harcourt, 1960); ——, *Social Behavior: Its Elementary Forms* (New York: Harcourt, 1961); Henry W. Riecken and George C. Homans, "Psychological Aspects of Social Structure," in Gardner Lindzey, *Handbook of Social Psychology* (Cambridge, Mass.: Addison-Wesley, 1954). These three sources provide a discussion of Homans's theory and its application to the research literature.

MIDDLE-RANGE THEORIES

A. Paul Hare, Edgar F. Borgatta, and Robert F. Bales (eds.), *Small Groups* (New York: Knopf, 1955).

Warren G. Bennis, Kenneth D. Benne, and Robert Chin (eds.), *The Planning of Change* (New York: Harper and Row, 1961).

Dorwin Cartwright and Alvin Zander (eds.), *Group Dynamics* (2d ed., Evanston, Ill.: Row, Peterson, 1960).

Chapter 4

The State of Empirical
Knowledge: Research Findings

We now turn to the other side of the coin of science—research findings. In this chapter the concrete will be emphasized, rather than the abstract, and observed behavior will be dealt with primarily in descriptive terms. By "descriptive terms" it is meant that the variables and concepts involved will not, generally, be as abstract as those considered in Chapter 3, though they will often be stated in hypothesis form.

It is tempting to organize these research findings around a theory or around a paradigm of the major concepts or emphases utilized in research. This will not be done partly because such discussions are available in the literature[1] and partly because the purpose of this chapter is to encourage both the recognition in everyday life of these findings and a more general approach to them. Thus, on the one hand, the reader will be encouraged to draw on his experience for added illustrations of the findings and, on the other hand, to speculate about applications of these findings to sociological interests which lie somewhat outside the boundaries of small groups as embodied in the theories reviewed in Chapter 3.

[1] See A. Paul Hare, *Handbook of Small Group Research* (New York: The Free Press of Glencoe, 1962); Gardner Lindzey, *Handbook of Social Psychology* (Cambridge, Mass.: Addison-Wesley, 1954), especially Chapters 6, 10, 11, 21, 22, and 24; Mary E. Roseborough, "Experimental Studies of Small Groups," *Psychological Bulletin*, 50, 1953, pp. 275-303.

Some research findings have already been embodied in the discussion of theories. All of these findings will not be repeated here, but it should be noted that they underlie a good deal of what has been said. The findings to be discussed here will be organized around four aspects of small groups: First, around the notion of similarity-dissimilarity, since "consciousness of kind and consciousness of difference"[2] seem to lie at the base of patterns of social relations. Second, around degrees of conformity, since conformity-individuality are current concerns of citizens and social scientists and find their way into research designs. Third, around the problem of authority, since leadership and influence are crucial aspects of group behavior. And fourth, around cohesion and productivity, since these are, either separately or together, the reasons for the existence of groups. The specific findings below will not be documented separately, but abstracts of relevant studies will be interspersed throughout the chapter. The abstracts are intended to serve several purposes. First, they provide some documentary evidence related to the discussion in the text. Second, they provide some idea of the problems involved in gathering and analyzing research on aspects of small-group behavior. Third, they illustrate a variety of approaches in theory, procedure, and results. These studies have been intentionally selected from among those available in the Bobbs-Merrill Reprint Series in the Social Sciences so that teachers and students may utilize the original reports of the studies. In addition, a selected bibliography will be presented at the end of the chapter.

SIMILARITY-DISSIMILARITY

The notion of similarity-dissimilarity is an aspect of a basic social phenomenon: the process of differentiating qualities and objects and differentially evaluating them (stratification). Differentiation does not necessarily lead to stratification, but stratifica-

---

[2] These terms are attributed to Franklin H. Giddings. See Robert Bierstedt, *The Social Order* (2d ed.; New York: McGraw-Hill, 1963), pp. 293-296 and 467-469.

tion presupposes differentiation. In a small group the recognition of similarity and dissimilarity between self and others is a key aspect of the broader process of differentiation, and evaluation of others in terms of positive and negative sentiments (liking and disliking) is a key aspect of the broader process of stratification.

When people first meet they form impressions of each other which may be favorable, neutral, or unfavorable. The sources of these impressions are still unclear, but three major sources have been located. The first source is *generalized attitudes toward a social object*. People have generalized attitudes toward many social objects, such as labor-union officials, conservatives, Negroes, armed-forces officers, and men who smoke cigars. These generalized attitudes are usually accompanied by feelings of liking or disliking, of attraction or repulsion.[3] When people meet strangers who possess characteristics that enable them to be placed in classes of social objects about which people have generalized attitudes, the feelings of liking or disliking toward the classes of social objects will usually be transferred to the particular strangers involved. This process of transference is greater when generalized attitudes are stereotypes, for then they tend to be absolute attitudes, that is, attitudes toward *all* labor-union officials.

The second source of initial impressions is *attitudes toward a significant other*. People have attitudes toward other persons who, for one reason or another, have been very important to them. These other persons may be one's parents, siblings, other relatives, a teacher, or some other person upon whom an individual has become dependent for the development and reinforcement of his conception of himself. When the relationship of a person to a significant other has contributed to that person's high self-esteem, he has positive sentiments toward the significant other, and when the relationship has contributed to that person's low

[3] The importance of liking and disliking, attraction and repulsion, has been advocated most vigorously by J. L. Moreno. See his "Foundations of Sociometry, an Introduction," *Sociometry*, 4, 1941, pp. 15-35, and his *Who Shall Survive?* (rev. ed.; Beacon, N.Y.: Beacon House, 1951).

self-esteem, he has negative sentiments toward the significant other. When people meet others who remind them of a significant other, they tend to transfer to such people their feelings of liking or disliking toward the significant other. This process is illustrated by the comment, "You know, you remind me of (a father, mother, brother, sister, close friend, etc.)," the unstated completion of which is, "Because of that similarity I hold toward you attitudes and feelings similar to those I hold toward that person."

The third source of initial impressions is *a person's level of self-esteem.* When a person's self-esteem is high he will be more apt to like others and to respond to others as individuals, less apt to engage in stereotyping. When a person's self-esteem is low he will be more apt to dislike others and to engage in stereotyping, less apt to respond to others as unique individuals. When a person sees in others those qualities which he dislikes in himself, he will tend to dislike the others. Part of the reason for this dislike is that such others remind him of his own weaknesses, and being reminded of his own weaknesses is uncomfortable to him. However, when a person perceives that others detect his weaknesses along with his strengths, he will tend to like them (see the abstract of Newcomb's study). Part of the reason for this liking is that if the others see a person's weaknesses and still like him or, at least, accept him as he is, he may feel that his weaknesses are not so bad after all.

If people like each other they will try to interact, and if they dislike each other they will try to avoid one another. Sentiment and interaction are directly related.[4] Further interaction may lead people to alter their sentiments toward each other in one of three ways. First, they may become disillusioned with each other and their liking may change to disliking and, as a consequence, interaction between them may drop off sharply. Second, they may find that their initial disliking was based on misconceptions

See George C. Homans, *The Human Group* (New York: Harcourt, 1950), and *Social Behavior: Its Elementary Forms* (New York: Harcourt, 1961).

of each other and further information may lead them to like each other and, thus, to increase the interaction between them. Third, further interaction may substantiate their initial sentiment and lead to increased interaction if they like each other or increased diligence in avoidance if they dislike each other. The effects of propinquity and similarity on the relation between sentiment and interaction are discussed in Newcomb's study (see the abstract).

The initial reaction and the effects of later reactions are complicated by the fact that people cannot respond to all the cues which others manifest nor can they hope always to interpret correctly the intent behind others' manifested behavior. Selective perception and the distortion of interpretation make it possible for perceptions to be self-sustaining, for people to maintain their initial reactions and to feel convinced that their first impressions were correct. People with low self-esteem are likely to perceive more selectively and to interpret the intent of others less correctly than people with high self-esteem. The people who have a high level of self-esteem are likely to perceive more cues manifested by others, to have more information on which to base an impression, and to interpret the intent of others more correctly. People with a high level of self-esteem are also more likely to change their impressions of others as they interact more with them.

The initial reaction may be sustained or modified by later reactions. These later reactions depend, in addition to the above three variables, on at least two other important variables: status-role and biography.[5] As people get to know each other better they learn more about the status-role positions they occupy, have occupied, or will likely occupy, and this social placement affects their sentiments toward each other. They also get to know each other as unique human beings, individuals each with a unique biography which may have elements leading to a feeling of

[5] See Alfred Schutz, "Common-Sense and Scientific Interpretation of Human Action," *Philosophy and Phenomenological Research*, 14, 1953, pp. 1-38; Peter L. Berger, *Invitation to Sociology: A Humanist Perspective* (Garden City, N.Y.: Doubleday, 1963).

ABSTRACT OF

THEODORE M. NEWCOMB, "The Prediction of Interpersonal Attraction," *American Psychologist*, 11, 1956, pp. 575-586.

PROBLEM

What are the relative contributions of propinquity and similarity to interpersonal attraction?

DESIGN

The author rented a house near the University of Michigan campus which could house seventeen men. He offered free rent to students transferring to Michigan from other universities, selecting seventeen men who did not know each other. In return for free rent the men agreed to spend four or five hours a week being interviewed by Newcomb and his assistants, filling out questionnaires, or participating in experiments.

FINDINGS

1. Roommates were more attracted to each other than to non-roommates in the house, and men living on each of the two floors were more attracted to others on their floor than to men on the other floor.

2. Men liked others who they perceived liked them or who, in fact, liked them.

3. Men were very accurate in their estimation of others' liking for them, and the degree of accuracy did not change much after the fourth day to the end of the school year even though some individuals came to be better liked and others less well liked.

4. A man liked those others best who saw him as he saw himself, and especially when they detected his weaknesses as well as his strengths.

5. Men who liked each other tended to agree (be similar) in their liking for other men and in their attitude toward important and relevant objects, such as the house, values, and other general kinds of objects.

similarity or dissimilarity. These additional effects, in combination with the three sources of initial impressions, seem to comprise the major factors involved in the nature of the sentiments people hold toward each other.

The relation of sentiment and interaction, though grossly a direct relation (increased positive sentiment and increased interaction are related), is in detail a set of four relations. (1) Initial positive sentiment leads to increased interaction, accompanied by later positive sentiments which lead to continued increased interaction up to some maximum point determined by other forces. (2) Initial positive sentiment leads to increased interaction, accompanied by later negative sentiments which lead to decreased interaction down to a minimum determined by other forces. (Even if a secretary dislikes her boss she has to interact some with him.) (3) Initial negative sentiment leads to decreased interaction (avoidance), accompanied by later negative sentiments which lead to continued or increased diligence in avoidance. (4) Initial negative sentiment leads to decreased interaction, accompanied by later positive sentiments which lead to increased interaction. After distinguishing between initial and later sentiments and presence or absence of interaction, the details of the sentiment-interaction hypothesis are still seen to support the gross statement—there is a direct relation. No account is taken here of the effects of an initial or later reaction of neutrality or indifference. It is plausible to assume that just as sentiments may be either positive or neutral or negative, so may interaction be desired or chance or avoided. A neutral sentiment would be accompanied by chance or haphazard interaction—neither sought out or encouraged nor avoided or discouraged.

The initial consciousness of kind or of difference establishes sentiments which affect the ensuing degree and kind of interaction. Perception of similarity, at least to some degree, encourages interaction which not only feeds back to sustain or modify the initial reactions, but also affects the general atmosphere (either cooperative or competitive) and the degree and kind of communication. A cooperative atmosphere typically accompanies similarity, a competitive atmosphere accompanies dissimilarity. So, too, active communication accompanies similarity, inactive communication accompanies dissimilarity.

Given similarity, high interaction, a cooperative atmosphere, and active communication, members of a group seek actively to influence each other. As their interaction increases, gradations of influence begin to emerge which, over time, lead to the development of agreement and to role differentiation. In such a group, influence attempts are high—the perception of similarity is tested and, when disagreement exists, a determined effort to resolve it takes place. The resolution typically is successful and the disagreements are resolved. And, furthermore, they are resolved not by compromise in which all members change their opinions, but by consensus, in which some members are won over by other members. The members change who are least committed to their position or least confident in their opinion, and those do not change who are most committed or most confident. Not only does this type of change take place, but a cooperative atmosphere plus the other characteristics discussed above lead also to increased role differentiation.

These findings about influence and role differentiation harbor some profound applications to social life. One is in connection with education. The often-supported notion that similarity and absence of role differentiation and presence of compromise are associated with successful group work and classroom teaching runs counter to research findings. The romantic notion of equality has obscured some of the characteristics of groups. The importance of similarity, cooperation, interaction, and communication were picked up, but not those of role differentiation and influence. In some circles, agreement by compromise seems valued over agreement by consensus. The contribution of dissimilarity under some conditions and the nature of cooperation, interaction, and communication have been confused. Active communication does not mean the same amount of communication, high interaction does not mean the same amount of interaction, and cooperation does not mean absence of disagreement. Slater's discussion of role differentiation (see the abstract) points up some of the roles which emerge in small groups, some of the qualities of behavior of persons who perform different roles, and the relation of these roles to consensus.

The confusion surrounding the characteristics of successful groups may be traced to some interpretations of democratic ideology which deny the existence of individual differences in ability and in motivation, of progressive education which emphasize adjustment and ignore problem solving, and of contemporary social life which ignore the importance of privacy and the positive values of urban living. A small group does not become successful by ignoring differences and demanding that members love one another and spend much time together (as proponents of the "togetherness" movement seem to advocate), but rather by expressing differences, by finding areas within which agreement can be reached, and by learning to live with disagreement. The democratic ideology involves safeguards for the minority, and successful small groups value differences as well as similarities and develop norms to guarantee the right to disagree, even after the final decision is made.

The discussion so far has emphasized the development of group characteristics and not the description of characteristics of an established group. In an established group which has achieved equilibrium, the same findings apply, but there are also some additional findings. First, status within the group tends to be correlated with external status. A man of high or low status in one group tends to have high or low status in other groups as well. Second, high status in a group (in terms of prestige of one's position) tends to be associated with high esteem (liking for the person). Esteem (liking or sociometric status) is not correlated one-to-one with status, however, since the best-liked person often has second or third status within the group—he is rarely the task leader of a group, but he is second or third high in status. In fact, in successful groups the best-liked person is often the lieutenant of the leader of the group who, though quite well liked,

ABSTRACT OF

PHILIP E. SLATER, "Role Differentiation in Small Groups"
American Sociological Review, 20, 1955, pp. 300-310.

PROBLEM

What kinds of differentiation in roles develop in small groups,
what are the similarities and differences of behavior of persons
performing different roles, and what are the differential effects of
psychological and sociological factors?

DESIGN

Twenty groups of three to seven men each met four times. At
each meeting they were given a case involving an administrative
problem and were instructed to discuss the case and decide why
the people described in the case were behaving as they did and
what action should be taken regarding the case. Their interaction
was recorded using Bales's set of categories. After the forty-min-
ute session they filled out a brief questionnaire asking them to
rank members (including themselves) on who contributed the
best ideas and on who did most to guide the discussion, and to
rank each member on how well the respondent liked him. At the
end of the fourth session they were also asked to rank members,
including themselves, on who stood out as a leader in the discussions.

FINDINGS

1. Persons who were liked best (popular) in the groups were
not usually ranked highest on ideas or guidance, and were not
the most active participators, so that a social-emotional specialist
(popular, best liked) emerged.

2. In the groups of high status consensus (groups whose members tended to agree with each other in their rankings), participation (ascribed to the man who talked most and toward whom
most comments were directed), and task ability (ascribed to persons highest on idea and guidance rankings) tend to be correlated,
so that one person emerged as the task-ability specialist.

3. In the groups of low status consensus, participation and task

ability tend to be uncorrelated, so that a participation specialist and a task-ability specialist emerged.

4. In the groups of high status consensus, the task specialist tended to emphasize problem-solving attempts (giving suggestions, opinions, and information) and the social-emotional specialist tended to emphasize reactions (both positive and negative reactions, such as showing agreement or disagreement, showing tension, and releasing tension).

5. In the groups of low status consensus, there was a lesser tendency for the participation specialist, the task-ability specialist, and the social-emotional specialist to emphasize a category of behavior.

6. In the groups of high status consensus, the task specialist and the social-emotional specialist interacted more with each other than either did with other members.

7. In the groups of low status consensus, the three specialists did not tend to interact more with each other than with other members.

8. In groups of high status consensus, sociological factors associated with developing an effective group seemed to predominate over the individual member's personality needs.

9. In the groups of low status consensus, a member's personality needs tended to predominate over the requirements of effective group action.

may also be the recipient of negative feelings. That is, members of the group may have ambivalent feelings toward the leader. (See the abstract of Slater's study.)

The differentiation and stratification which take place in a small group not only establish the roles of task leader and social-emotional leader (best-liked person), but other roles which may be described as the ignored, the nice guy, and the rejected. Blau's concepts of *attractiveness* and *approachability* (see Chapter 2) may be used to discuss the differentiation and stratification which take place. The *task leader* of a group is highly attractive in that he possesses skills or characteristics which the group values highly, but he is not highly approachable. He must not be unapproachable, however, for being so would result in his being too great a threat to other members. The *social-emotional leader* is highly approachable in that others feel he is one to whom they can complain, fret, show affection, or in other ways express their feelings, and he is more attractive than other group members though not quite so highly attractive as the task leader. He must be fairly highly attractive for if he were not he would not be so highly valued. The reason his high approachability is valued is that he is also fairly attractive and, thus, can influence the task leader. Members of a small group who are *ignored* are usually inactive, and they are perceived by others as neither attractive nor unattractive, approachable nor unapproachable— they are unknown objects. The *nice guys* in a group are perceived as attractive and approachable, not so highly so as the task leader or the social-emotional leader, but enough so that their membership and contributions are valued. The *rejected* is a person who is perceived as highly unattractive and/or highly unapproachable. He is perceived as unattractive if he possesses no skills or characteristics valued by the group or if he possesses skills or characteristics which are disliked by group members. He is perceived as unapproachable if he suppresses or inhibits most of his reactions, manifests inconsistent or confusing behavior, or is openly hostile to members of the group.

CONFORMITY

People are usually disposed to conform to the norms which govern the situations they find themselves in. When people violate norms, this violation may mean that they misunderstand the norms involved or that they disagree with them. If they misunderstand the norms involved, clarification of the norms may lead to conformity. If, however, they disagree with the norms, even after clarifying their misunderstanding, they may still violate them. Continued violation of norms in a situation may exist under one or both of two conditions: (1) If the norms in a situation are contrary to more general norms a person holds or contrary to the norms of some other reference group important to a person, he will likely violate them. (2) If a nonconformist finds support from at least one other member of the group, or from the imagined approval of another person or group, he will likely continue to violate the norms. (See the abstract of Deutsch and Gerard's study on social influences on judgment.)

Though the mechanisms involved in the conformity process are complex some of their salient features are fairly clear. Perception of similarity is related to conformity—if a person perceives others in a group to be like him (and if he likes himself), then he is apt to conform to the group's norms since so doing will be his "natural" inclination. But if he perceives some dissimilarity, then he is apt to take refuge in his desire to avoid mental or emotional conflict and seek to maintain his sense of personal integrity by nonconformity. If his nonconformity to the norms of a group means conformity to the norms of the broader culture, then he may be quite determined to maintain his deviance. He can not only imagine approval from the generalized other, from most people in society, but he may also imagine approval from members of other reference groups whose norms are consistent with general social norms. The rate buster[6] in industry typifies this mechanism. He deviates from the production

---

[6] Melville Dalton, "The Industrial 'Rate-Buster': A Characterization," *Applied Anthropology*, 7, 1948, pp. 5-18.

MORTON DEUTSCH and HAROLD B. GERARD, "A Study of Normative and Informational Social Influences upon Individual Judgment," *Journal of Abnormal and Social Psychology,* 51, 1955, pp. 629-636.

PROBLEM

To study the separate and combined effects of information and group norms on judgment.

DESIGN

The basic experimental situation involved bringing four persons together in a room and asking each of them to judge which of three lines drawn on a card was closest in length to a fourth line on the card. Two basic experimental conditions were used: (1) Face to face condition: four persons (three of whom were stooges and instructed to answer incorrectly on most of the cards) sat at a table, a card was shown, and they announced their judgment with the naive subject (S) announcing his decision third in sequence, preceded by two stooges and followed by one stooge. (2) Anonymous condition: four naive persons were brought into a room together and then each placed in a cubicle so that they were aware of each other's presence but unable to see or talk with each other and unable to detect who was making which judgment; in this condition, judgments were indicated by pressing a button which lit up a light corresponding to the indicated choice; all four Ss were privately informed they were S number three and the others one, two, and four; the experimenter made judgments for the assumed Ss one, two, and four from a master panel, representing electronic stooges comparable to the stooges in condition one. Further conditions were introduced in either or both of the face-to-face and anonymous conditions: offering a prize to the five groups in the anonymous condition who made the fewest incorrect judgments; in both basic conditions, one sequence of 18 cards was run with each card visually present while judgments were being made and a second sequence with each card removed (hence Ss had to rely on their memory); in some cases the Ss wrote their private judgments down on paper or on a Magic Pad before announcing their judgment, and in some of these cases the papers were thrown away and in other cases the Ss were informed that the experimenter would collect them so as to have a record of the S's private judgment before announcing his public judgment.

FINDINGS

1. More errors were made in the groups competing for a prize than in the noncompeting groups, both in the anonymous condition. That is, the Ss tended to agree with the electronic stooges, even when the S's own private judgment was correct and the electronic stooges' judgments were incorrect. The Ss had no reason not to believe the judgments were being made by the other three Ss. This finding supports the hypothesis that normative influence stems largely from a group and overrides personal judgment.

2. More errors were made by Ss in the face-to-face condition than in the anonymous condition.

3. The effects of making an individual judgment prior to announcing a public judgment were to reduce the number of errors made, and the effects of making a judgment by memory were to increase the number of errors made.

4. The results strongly support the general propositions that persons tend to rely initially on their own judgment, that they look to others for agreement or disagreement, that when a person disagrees with others he is likely to accept their judgment unless some process occurs which leads him to rely more on his own judgment, and that a group can undermine or can reinforce a person's tendency to rely on his own judgment (in groups where a group norm developed which placed value on each individual's judgment, the group reinforced the individual).

norms (informal) of his work group, but in the direction of general social norms (to be productive, a hard worker, a good provider for his family). He may be lonesome at work, but be considered the pillar of his family, church, lodge, or community.

The tendency of people to avoid mental or emotional conflict, to ignore (as the rate buster does) the norms of a group of which they are members, or to maintain conformity to a group's norms in the face of strong counter normative pressures, has been developed as a major proposition of a theory of human behavior. Festinger[7] (a student of Lewin) in the theory of cognitive dissonance argues that people strive to maintain consonance and to avoid dissonance in their mental and emotional lives. This tendency is held to be so strong that when people are thoroughly integrated into a deviant group, evidence contrary to their norms or disconfirmation of their predictions will result in stronger beliefs or conformity to their norms.[8]

When people perceive their own dissimilarity they are usually uncomfortable about it. They may decrease their discomfort by feeling that they are conforming to more important norms and may become even more obstinate in their nonconformity. If they do so, they are most apt to seek support—first from other deviants in the group (if such exist), and then from others outside the group. They may seek acceptance or solace in other groups whose norms are personally more compatible, or from persons (real or historical figures) who hold such counter norms. Failing this, they may become the brooding, silent members or indignantly leave the group.

But nonconformists may find little solace in thus leaving, since others are not in their immediate presence. They may have little confidence in their opinions and be ready to change. Their low confidence and high readiness to change may also mean that they are relatively silent, having little to say. If so, others in the

---

[7] Leon Festinger, *A Theory of Cognitive Dissonance* (Evanston, Ill.: Row, Peterson, 1957).

[8] Leon Festinger, Henry W. Riecken, Jr., and Stanley Schachter, *When Prophecy Fails* (Minneapolis: University of Minnesota Press, 1956).

group may direct communication to them in an attempt to influence their opinions, and are likely to be successful. If the deviant perceives a fairly high degree of similarity between himself and others in the group, he is more likely to feel that he has been mistaken, that somehow he has misinterpreted the norms he has violated, and that change will be in his own interests as well as approved by others in the group.

If others in the group seek to change a deviant's opinions, they are in effect saying that they would like to accept him and not reject him. If he wants to be accepted and if change does little violence to his personal integrity he has little to lose by changing. However, if he wants to be accepted and doesn't change he may be rejected since attempts to influence deviants increase up to a point, but with continued failure the conformers eventually give up. (See the abstract of Schachter's study.) If a deviant is not too sure about his nonconformity, he may feel that he had better give in before this point is reached—otherwise he may find himself established as a nonconformist. Deviants are usually rejected, and most people do not enjoy rejection. Given the self-sustaining nature of typifications, such identification may then be exceedingly difficult to change.

The fact that a person is a deviant in one group has other consequences as well. He will also probably be rejected by outsiders who have some familiarity with the group, unless, of course, their norms are consistent with the deviant's reasons for nonconformity. In this latter case the deviant's nonconformity to one group means conformity to another group (a reference group for him). And what better position for a group to be in than to have a member (or sympathetic nonmember) be a nonconforming member of another group? This may mean access to "inside dope" which would otherwise be unavailable. And, equally, what greater threat to a group's security than to have a nonconformist who, people may suspect, is a conformist to some other group?

Conformity and nonconformity are not matters of black and white. Some degree of deviance may not only be tolerated, it

ABSTRACT OF

STANLEY SCHACHTER, "Deviation, Rejection, and Communi-cation," *Journal of Abnormal and Social Psychology*, 46, 1951, pp. 190-207.

PROBLEM

To study the process of communication within a small group directed at a member of the group who deviates from the group standard, the effects of cohesiveness and relevance of the group standard on the process of communication, and the degree of re-jection of deviates.

DESIGN

The researchers recruited male college students to participate in the experiment. Thirty-two groups of eight to ten members each were studied. In each group there were three stooges— students who were in collusion with the experimenters. One of the stooges was *modal* who agreed with the position the majority of the naive subjects took on the task. A second stooge was a *slider* who disagreed with the group's position at first but gradu-ally shifted his position until he was modal at the end. A third stooge was a *deviate* who disagreed with the group's position throughout the meeting. Each group was given a story about a young delinquent to read, and asked whether they thought the delinquent should be treated with love and understanding or should be punished. All the groups took a position more toward love and understanding, and the slider at first and the deviate throughout took the position of strong punishment. Using a schedule of categories, the researchers observed the groups and then asked group members to fill out a questionnaire and answer some interview questions at the end.

FINDINGS

1. Communication was directed toward the deviate and slider to change their positions. As the slider agreed more with the group, communication toward him decreased.
2. Communication toward the deviate fell off toward the end

of the meeting in the groups of high cohesiveness and high relevance. (High relevance refers to those groups in which the issue was relevant to the group, low relevance to those groups in which the issue was irrelevant to the group.)

3. These effects above were greater in high-cohesiveness groups than in low-cohesiveness groups, and greater in groups of high relevance than in groups of low relevance.

4. The slider was not rejected by members of the group, but the deviate was. However, some members had stronger sentiments of rejection of the deviate than others.

may even be desirable. (See the abstract of Dentler and Erikson's discussion of the functions of deviance.) Since status and degree of conformity are directly related, differentiation of status may also mean that differentiation of conformity is desirable. What better test of a man's low status than his low degree of conformity? Or of his high status than his high degree of conformity? And what better guarantee of potential for growth or change than the presence of some disagreement over the importance of group norms? Thus members of groups typically settle into a routine of established degrees of conformity which come to be expected of them and, hence, are no longer targets of influence.

Conformity may also be a means for status mobility. A low-status person may increase his degree of conformity as he seeks to raise his status. In a small group, a change in conformity by a member is a threat to the established hierarchy and is typically met with reaction aimed at reestablishing the routinized degree of conformity. And, since changes in identity are not expected and are resisted, a successful change is most apt to occur only if the nature of the change in identity can somehow be dramatized. Dramatizing change, however, is difficult in a small group since there are few institutionalized procedures for dramatization. There are no coming-out parties, puberty rites, graduation ceremonies, or formal weddings. There are, of course, some procedures which develop—initiation ceremonies, election of officers, and the like. But these procedures are not usually in the control of the deviant—he cannot elect to hold them or engage in them, but must wait to be invited. And if the members of the group will not accept his avowed or attempted change, how can he expect to be invited?

The direct relation between status and conformity, however, obscures some important details. Although high-status persons are often seen as high conformers, they are also given more leeway in conformity. Thus their high conformity may be more in the nature of potential and capacity than fact. They can conform and their ability to conform may be accepted, but they may also be expected to lead the direction of change or, at least, to have

ABSTRACT OF

ROBERT A. DENTLER and KAI T. ERIKSON, "The Functions of Deviance in Groups," *Social Problems*, 7, 1959, pp. 98-107.

PROBLEM

To account for the existence and apparent importance of deviance in groups.

DESIGN

The authors develop three propositions which summarize a great deal of the research literature and illustrate the relevance of these propositions with data gathered in a study of ten Quaker work projects and a study of basic-training squads in the United States Army from which eleven persons were later hospitalized as schizophrenics.

FINDINGS

1. "Groups tend to induce, sustain, and permit deviant behavior."
2. "Deviant behavior functions in enduring groups to help maintain group equilibrium."
3. "Groups will resist any trend toward alienation of a member whose behavior is deviant."

Quaker work projects which were most successful in achieving their objectives also had the highest proportions of isolates and some of these were low-ranking deviants. Other group members worked hard to understand and accept the deviants, and generally the deviants conformed to some degree to what the groups considered some of their basic rules. The other group members' concern for accepting the deviant and attempting to change him functioned to reinforce their commitment to the group. In some cases where the deviant finally left the group, other group members felt guilty and saddened by his departure.

In basic-training squads, members developed a tolerance and a place for deviant members—the deviants often being referred to as "our teddy bear," "our pet," "mascot," "little brother," or "toy."

The deviant's duties were usually performed by others and they became very protective of him. When the deviant was finally removed and hospitalized as a schizophrenic, squad members were disturbed and angry, insisting that it was all right for him to be in the squad, that he was not ill and should not be hospitalized, and the like.

gained the right to deviate occasionally if they so wish. They do not have to prove that they accept the norms, and, indeed, may know better than others that complete conformity is, at times, unwise. Conformity to norms, to the high-status person, may be seen more clearly as a means to achieving the objectives of the group. Whereas middle-status members may define conformity as an end in itself, low-status members may accept their expected low degree of conformity. On the other hand, a low-status person who thinks he is on the verge of losing membership in the group may be the highest conformer of all as he seeks to avoid abolition and to affirm his desire and capacity to be an accepted member. Thus it may be that the relation between status and conformity is direct under some circumstances and curvilinear under others.

The fact that high-status members often conform closely to the norms of a group may be due to the fact that they are often the most influential, and may be the most influential in deciding what the norms are to be. Thus the personal integrity of high-status members, their degree of acceptance of general cultural norms, the compatibility of the group's norms with the norms of other reference groups for them, are all apt to be consistent—at least as consistent as the high-status members are able to achieve. If high-status members recognize that some inconsistency is likely to be present and that change over time is probable, their taste for nonconformity (leeway) is also likely to be high. But their nonconformity is not apt to be perceived as capricious, threatening, or antagonistic—they have something to lose, whereas the low-status person has little to lose. And since he has little to lose, his motives may be suspect.

Status and conformity are related in still another way. Members of groups seem to accord esteem (one ingredient of status) to others on two grounds: their personal feelings and the perceived degree of conformity. When a member does exceedingly well at something valued by the group or by the environing society, he is accorded esteem even if it means some sacrifice to others in the group. Thus in competitive groups there is a tendency to accord esteem to a highly productive person even though his success may mean some loss to others. On the other hand, there is a tendency to accord esteem to others of similar status, since personally one may like or feel comfortable with a peer. It may be that when one chooses to work with a person of low productivity in a competitive group he does so to enhance his chances of being successful in the two-person competition. Choosing to work with a person of low productivity, however, may also lead to guilt feelings and the chooser may then accord esteem to a highly productive person to denote that justice is being served.

AUTHORITY[9]

Members of a group who possess authority may acquire it through either ascription, appointment, or personal achievement. The ascribed leader possesses his authority through divine right or traditional decree. (Ascription via inheritance, as to kings, is the most obvious.) Just as members of a group in such a case have nothing to say about the appointment, neither can they change it. For this reason an ascribed leader's position is not threatened, except by revolution, and the problems he faces are quite different, in many ways, from those that confront appointed or earned leaders. Since ascribed leadership is rarely found in small groups (though ascriptive factors are related to leadership) nothing more will be said about it here.

The differences between appointed and earned authority are very important. Their importance stems from the fact that appointed leaders must usually earn authority, at least to some degree, since their appointment may also be revoked. (See the abstract of Whyte's study on corner boys.) Also, earned leaders must often acquire appointment in order to legitimize their authority. Because both appointment and earning tend to converge, the problems involved in this convergence become crucial. Appointed leaders may earn authority in three major ways—first,

[9] Much of the following discussion draws heavily on Homans's discussion of authority in *Social Behavior, op. cit.* in note 4.

they may risk all immediately and seek to demonstrate that they are capable of earning their authority. If they succeed they have, by one stroke, added important dimensions to their authority since they gain both legitimate authority and accepted authority within the group. Newly commissioned officers in the armed forces (especially in stress situations) may risk all immediately. But if the appointed leader is wrong, and if he makes a mistake at the outset, he has demonstrated his inability to earn authority. If he cannot earn authority, the legitimacy of his appointed authority is questioned by his subordinates and by his superiors. If he succeeds, all concerned laud him; but if he fails his superiors may agree that he is a fool, and his subordinates that he is a fake.

Second, appointed leaders may earn authority through a slow process of accretion in which the appointed leader maintains some control over the perception of success. Thus the appointed leader may begin earning authority through making decisions unknown to the group and, if they work out well, he then announces them. If they do not work out well, he doesn't announce them and no one is the wiser. Or he may begin with relatively unimportant decisions, delaying his own opinion until he is on safe ground—this way he ensures acceptance. Better, he may first find out whether an action he is thinking about can be carried off, and, if he is quite sure it can, he proposes it, along with the idea that it may be exceedingly difficult to achieve but that he will do his best. Then, when it succeeds, he has earned a nice increment of authority—it was difficult, but he somehow managed to carry it off. Throughout the process of earning authority the appointed leader values secrecy—especially secrecy regarding the perception of success. Since failure on his part may jeopardize his position, and may do so quite capriciously (without justification), he is apt to desire as great a control as possible over others' awareness of what he is doing.

Third, an appointed leader may earn authority by frankly exposing his intent and desire to earn authority. If he can do so, this procedure is probably more successful than the immediate gambit in which he may fail and be unable to recover, or the

ABSTRACT OF

WILLIAM FOOTE WHYTE, "Corner Boys: A Study of Clique Behavior," *American Journal of Sociology,* 46, 1941, pp. 647-664.

PROBLEM

To study groupings of corner boys in a slum area of a city, the relative rank or position within the groupings, some of the qualities of the interaction among group members, and some of the functions of the group leaders.

DESIGN

The author moved into the area and became a participant observer of the various groupings. He relied mostly on observation and informal interviewing, making notes later in the privacy of his room. He lived in the area more than a year and spent most of his waking hours observing and talking with corner boys (the corner boys were in their twenties or early thirties and some were married). He came to rely heavily on one corner boy, a leader of a grouping, for information and for reaction to the findings and conclusions he developed.

FINDINGS

1. Repeated observation of people in a permanent social situation can enable one to locate enduring subgroups which function as groupings outside of that situation.

2. Position (rank or status) in a group is directly related to the degree of origination of action for the group.

3. A group can be effectively influenced by influencing the top two or three persons in the status hierarchy.

4. Once the status hierarchy of group members is established much energy goes into maintaining members' relative positions to each other.

5. Group members develop a subtle and complex system of mutual obligations and reciprocities.

6. Position in the group is inversely related to violating or failing to discharge mutual obligations.

7. In-group cohesion and out-group hostility are directly related.

8. Interaction and similarity of position in group are directly related.

9. Position in the group is directly related to resourcefulness (knowing what to do), fair-mindedness, and skill in things valued by the group.

slow accretion in which his failures may be exposed. To be straightforward takes a lot of ego strength, since he is almost certain to encounter failures and he wants to avoid reacting defensively. This is the style of leadership typically called democratic or permissive leadership, and represents a combination of the immediate gambit and the slow accretion. This style is probably the most difficult, however, since it entails long-run success or failure. If a leader risks all immediately and fails, he can blame chance. If he finds his well-kept secrets exposed, he can blame his unprincipled enemies. But if over time he is unable to earn authority through openness, whom can he blame but himself?

The leader (or high-status member) typically is involved in an exchange situation[10] with the members of his group. (See the abstract of Whyte's study on restaurants.) He does them favors, and they return in kind. But his position typically means that he must be ahead of the game, he must be one-up over the other members, he must be capable of giving more than he receives. Hence he usually finds himself in the strange predicament of holding promissory notes from the other members which have no specific values (they are signed blank checks) but which cannot be cashed in without entailing further favors on his part. And, with each added favor he gives, something must be returned for the other members do not like to have the potential value of the promissory note too high. The day may come when all members decide to pay up their debts in order to establish equality (possibly as a prelude to change) or to disband the group.

COHESION AND PRODUCTIVITY

Most people can think of groups of which they have been proud or ashamed to be members. Proud when the group has

---

[10] Alvin W. Gouldner, "The Norm of Reciprocity: A Preliminary Statement," *American Sociological Review*, 25, 1960, pp. 161-178; George C. Homans, "Human Behavior as Exchange," *American Journal of Sociology*, 63, 1958, pp. 597-606; ——, *Social Behavior, op. cit.* in note 4, especially Chapters 1, 3, and 4.

ABSTRACT OF

WILLIAM FOOTE WHYTE, "The Social Structure of the Restaurant," *American Journal of Sociology*, 54, 1949, pp. 302-310.

PROBLEM

To study the roles of employees in a restaurant, their interaction with each other, and the effects on interaction of status, sex, and layout and equipment.

DESIGN

The author and four assistants made interview or participant observation studies of twelve restaurants in Chicago over a period of fourteen months, with at least one researcher spending from one to four months in each restaurant.

FINDINGS

1. Absence of tension in waitresses and their efficiency were directly related to originating contact with customers. If a customer got the jump on the waitress, the waitress became tense and her efficiency suffered.

2. An important function of the supervisor was to help out the waitress, especially in rush periods, so that she maintained control of the customer.

3. Work flow was smoothest when persons of higher status originated work for others of lower status, and friction developed when persons of lower status originated work for others of higher status. An important function of supervisors was to detect when a subordinate needed the supervisor's help, and to offer it before it had to be requested.

4. When persons of lower status originated work for persons of higher status (for example, as when waitresses necessarily gave orders to cooks), friction was decreased by making the process as impersonal as possible.

5. Sex functioned primarily as a status factor: men generally had higher status than women and men generally held the more prestigeful jobs in the restaurant.

6. The formal structure set limits on human relations, and

face-to-face interaction determined the specific patterns of behavior.

7. All persons and interpersonal relations in a given group formed an interdependent system, so that a change in any one affected others as well.

meant something special to them, when it was able to hold together in the face of danger. Or proud when it accomplished a
difficult task, or won first prize in a competition. And sometimes
proud when a group both meant something special and worked
very effectively and successfully.

On the other hand, people have also been ashamed when they
failed to develop any sense of commitment to a group, or when
a group fell apart when confronted with some threat or pressure.
Or they have felt ashamed when the group failed to achieve its
objectives, was unable to complete a task in time, or clearly came
up with a makeshift and shoddy product. When a group has
neither meant much to people nor been productive, they may
try to forget the experience as soon as they can.

Cohesion refers to this quality of a group which includes individual pride, commitment, meaning, as well as the group's
stick-togetherness, ability to weather crises, and ability to maintain itself over time. *Productivity* refers to the group's ability to
work effectively and successfully, and to the willingness of members to do their jobs, no matter how onerous. Cohesion and productivity, as implied above, are related in complex ways. In some
cases, cohesion and productivity are directly related—the higher
the cohesion of a group, the higher its productivity. But sometimes a group's cohesion may be low though its productivity is
high, or its cohesion may be high though its productivity is low.
(See the abstract of Bavelas's study on communication, morale,
and productivity.) High productivity may be achieved when a
group is short-lived and composed of dissimilar but productive
members. Who has not been surprised by the disclosure that a
productive group was also riven with interpersonal hostility? Or
found an explanation for the first loss of an undefeated basket-
ball team in jealousy and grandstanding among the players?
High cohesion may develop when a group comes to value interpersonal warmth more than work output. What does it matter
if a group turns out ten instead of twenty television sets so long
as camaraderie is maintained? There seem to be some circumstances where there is an inverse relation between cohesion and
productivity.

ABSTRACT OF

ALEX BAVELAS, "Communication Patterns in Task-Oriented Groups," *Journal of the Acoustical Society of America*, 22, 1950, pp. 725-730.

PROBLEM

To develop a number of patterns of communication among members of a small group and to study the properties and effects of the different patterns.

DESIGN

Four logical patterns of communication among five persons were developed. Experimental groups of five subjects each were recruited and each group solved several problems in succession utilizing one or another of the five patterns. Each member of a five-person group was handed a card by the experimenter on which five geometric symbols were drawn. Only one symbol was common to all the cards of the five group members. A member could communicate to one, two, three, or four other members, depending on the pattern of communication his group had to use and on his position in that pattern. The problem was to decide which symbol was common to all five cards. Six symbols were used: five of these symbols were common to four of the cards, and one to all five. The patterns of communication were the *circle*, in which each person could communicate to the person to his left and to the person to his right so that the pattern was a closed circle; the *line*, in which three persons could communicate to the right and to the left, but one end person could communicate only to the right and the other end person only to the left so that the pattern was not closed; the *star*, in which four persons each could communicate only to the fifth and he could communicate with all four others; and the *Y*, in which two persons could communicate both to their left and their right and three persons were at the ends of communication channels and could only communicate to their left or to their right, so that the pattern was not closed. The groups were timed as to speed of solution of the problem, counts were made of errors during

the solving and of incorrect completions of the task, and members were interviewed and filled out questionnaires after the task to gather information on satisfaction, recognition of leadership, and other attitudes and sentiments.

FINDINGS

1. The *Y* pattern group had fewest errors and solved the problem fastest. Leadership emerged clearly as that person who was in the most central position (the position to which or through which most information flowed.) The *star* and *line* pattern groups were intermediate, and the *circle* pattern group had most errors, was slowest in solving the problem, and had the least clearly recognized leadership (logically, no person in the circle pattern is in a more central position than the others.)

2. The *circle* pattern had the highest morale, the *Y* pattern the lowest, and the *star* and *line* patterns intermediate.

3. Persons in central positions (emergent leaders) had highest satisfaction, while persons in peripheral (end) positions had lowest satisfaction.

4. After many successive trials, leadership emerged in the *circle* pattern and its speed increased.

There appear to be still other conditions under which there is a curvilinear relation between cohesion and productivity. In this case, groups with low cohesion have low productivity, those with medium cohesion have high productivity, and those with high cohesion have medium or low productivity. The low-cohesion groups are stymied in their productive efforts by inability to cooperate, and the high-cohesion groups value interpersonal warmth more than work output. As in the case of status and conformity, the effect is similar but the reasons are different.

Groups which develop medium or high cohesion also develop norms governing productivity, as is clearly demonstrated in research which shows that *within groups,* cohesion and the degree of variability in the productivity of members is inverse—in high-cohesion groups, members tend to produce like amounts, but in low cohesion groups, they tend to produce dissimilar amounts. The same research has demonstrated that *between groups,* differences in productivity are directly related to cohesion—groups of high cohesion tend to produce dissimilar amounts, but groups of low-cohesion produce similar amounts. These two findings support the idea that the key to the relation between cohesion and productivity lies in the nature of the norms developed by the group. (See the abstract of the study by Schachter and others, on cohesiveness and productivity.)

In groups of low cohesion, norms governing productivity are either not developed or not enforceable. Thus group pressure or influence is not marshaled either in support of or in opposition to the larger organization's (or society's) norms of production. In groups of medium cohesion, norms governing productivity are developed and enforced. But since the group has only medium cohesion, it may be unable to enforce restrictive norms effectively or, for that matter, inspire effort beyond what is ordinarily required. Its productivity may be high, though not so high as in a group of high cohesion whose own group norms support the norms of the organization and/or society. And, finally, a group of high cohesion is able to enforce conformity to its productivity norms whether

ABSTRACT OF

STANLEY SCHACHTER, NORRIS ELLERTSON, DOROTHY McBRIDE, and DORIS GREGORY, "An Experimental Study of Cohesiveness and Productivity," *Human Relations*, 4, 1951, pp. 229-238.

PROBLEM

Will attempts to influence members toward high or low productivity be more effective in high-cohesion than in low-cohesion groups?

DESIGN

Several groups of three persons were given a task. The three persons were brought into an experimental room and led to believe they would be working together on a task of cutting out cardboard squares, gluing them on boards, and coloring them to produce checkerboards. Each member was placed in a separate room and each was instructed to cut out squares, being led to believe a second was gluing and a third coloring. Members were told they could communicate to each other by writing notes, with the experimenter delivering them. In fact, the experimenter collected the notes and distributed prearranged notes in order to induce greater productivity in half of the groups of three and less productivity in the other half. Half of the groups of three were also told, individually, that they would like each other and would work well together (inducing high cohesiveness), and the other half that they would probably not like each other and not work very well together (inducing low cohesiveness). Thus there were four conditions: high cohesiveness and increased productivity, low cohesiveness and decreased productivity, high cohesiveness and decreased productivity, and low cohesiveness and increased productivity.

FINDINGS

1. The members of groups where attempts were made to increase productivity did, in fact, increase their productivity, and

there was little difference between the high-cohesion and low-cohesion groups.

2. The members of groups where attempts ,were made to decrease productivity did so only in the high-cohesion groups, with the low-cohesion groups varying their productivity very little.

3. The results generally support the hypothesis that cohesion (attractiveness of a group to its members) is directly related to the degree of member influence on each other, and the direction of influence determines the productivity of a group. High-cohesion groups will be more successful than low-cohesion groups in increasing or reducing productivity.

they are in support of or in opposition to the productivity norms of the organization or society. And since in a large organization a good deal of variability in personal and social qualities is to be expected some groups are apt to develop supportive norms and others restrictive norms. Consequently, the average productivity of high-cohesion groups would depend on the distribution of such groups between supportive and restrictive orientations. In addition, as was noted above, a high-cohesion group may value interpersonal warmth more than work output and, even if its norms are supportive, it may depress its potential productivity.

There is an important extension of the ideas above to industrial and educational settings. If management could be assured that a group's norms would be supportive, then it would be desirable to encourage the development of high cohesion. However, even in the case of a high-cohesion group with supportive norms, there is no guarantee that the group would be a consistently high producer. It would have the *capacity* to be highly productive, but it would also have the capacity to depress productivity if it so chose. And it might choose to do so if it felt that the demands placed on it were unreasonable. The fact that it had high cohesion would mean that some group effort would have to be directed toward maintaining interpersonal warmth. Consequently, its productivity rate might not be a smoothly high one but a rate marked by cycles of extremely high productivity followed by low productivity.

This possibility suggests that a distinction ought to be made between average productivity and reserve productivity. There may be a curvilinear relation between cohesion and *average* productivity, but a direct relation between cohesion and *reserve* productivity. High-cohesion groups would be expected to have lower average productivity than medium-cohesion groups (both because of the counterbalance of supportive and restrictive norms, and because of the energy devoted to maintaining high cohesion), but to have higher reserve productivity than medium-cohesion groups. In an emergency, a high-cohesion group with

supportive norms would be able to produce more than is ordinarily required, even though its average productivity might
not be the highest.

The notion of reserve productivity is also related to the educational setting. Teachers (and students) deplore the bright
student who does not turn in his weekly papers on time but who
makes an A on the final examination. The teacher feels dis-
appointed, angry, or challenged by this performance, though the
other students may feel only a sense of some injustice or frus-
tration. The same type of performance is often noted in the case
of a group of students working together on a class project. The
teacher and the group may agree that the group has a high potential, but that potential may not be realized until realistic pressure is applied. The group may not feel that weekly progress
reports or routine activities are valuable or that their expectation
is a realistic pressure. Their final product, however, may be
imaginative and meaningful. If the educational goal is memoriza-
tion (and this is sometimes a necessary and desirable goal), average productivity may be the appropriate measure of success. But
if the educational goal is creativity (learning how to think, applying material to other situations, and the like), then reserve productivity may be the more appropriate criterion. Similarly, if
several students are working together as a group and they are
encouraged to develop high cohesion, then the teacher should be
prepared to expect the possible existence of reserve rather than
average productivity and govern his demands accordingly. High
cohesion is purchased at the costs of relinquishing some control
by the teacher and of modifying his expectations. These modifications do not mean that only a final product should be demanded—periodical products can still be demanded, but care
must be exercised to avoid the perception that such demands are
routine or that they occur so frequently that they become matters of habit rather than thought.

The notion of reserve productivity is also related to the nature
of individual satisfaction. If the generalizations from behavioral

psychology regarding constant-ratio versus variable-ratio reward[11] are correct, then variable-ratio reward is related to reserve productivity and innovative learning. If a rat is given a food pellet every time he pushes a lever (constant-ratio reward), his learning can be extinguished much faster than if he is given a pellet some times but not other times (variable-ratio reward). If we can assume that under a constant-ratio reward the learning is more habituated than under a variable-ratio reward and that there is more searching behavior under a variable-ratio reward, then providing a variable-ratio reward should lead to innovative learning and reserve productivity. Surprise quizzes and periodical (their frequency is a function of content and other things) papers or exams would be consistent with these ideas. But so too would leeway and emphasis on the final product. In fact, don't teachers give their best students more leeway in conforming to expectations than other students? Giving leeway to one's best students is partly to be expected on the basis of the relation between status and conformity, but it may also be related to something like the idea of reserve productivity, variable-ratio reward, and innovative learning. At any rate, individual satisfaction may be higher (at least for some people) under conditions of variable-ratio reward and reserve productivity where the emphasis is placed on certain crucial outputs rather than on routine outputs. Thus individual satisfaction, like cohesion, may be rather complexly related to productivity. Not only may A students not always be satisfied with their performance, but D students may sometimes be delighted that they did not fail.

CONCLUSION

Some of the findings of research on small groups have been surveyed in this chapter. Some major propositions and some modifying conditions have been discussed around the topics of similarity-dissimilarity as an aspect of differentiation and stratification; conformity and individuality; authority, leadership, and

[11] See Homans, *Social Behavior, op. cit.* in note 4, especially Chapter 2.

influence; and cohesion and productivity. Abstracts of nine research studies have been included to call attention to evidence supporting the discussion and to the types of research on small groups which are being conducted. Some implications of findings of small group studies on broader social phenomena (in industry and education) have been discussed.

The propositions in this chapter should be compared with the propositions derived from the theories presented in Chapter 3. To what extent can these research findings be predicted by logically deriving similar propositions from theory? To what extent are more general statements of these findings consistent with theory?

These findings should also be related to personal experiences, for in this way one is better able to judge the effects of modifying conditions, to develop powers of observation and interpretation, and to evaluate research studies.

Finally, the reader should keep in mind that what he reads here (or elsewhere, for that matter) must be filtered through his *critical judgment*—a judgment informed both by the attitude of daily life and by the scientific attitude.

Selected Bibliography for Chapter 4

It is difficult to select a small number of the numerous studies which have been conducted on small groups or on factors affecting behavior in small groups. The studies already cited in this chapter, in the preceding chapters, and in the chapter to come represent a selection which seems to parallel the text. Thirteen other studies are listed below which seem to round out topics not already referenced but discussed in the text. These are not meant to be exhaustive but to be a selection for purposes of becoming introduced to the field of small-group research. The reader who wishes to pursue the literature further should consult the following journals: *American Journal of Sociology, American Sociological Review, Human Relations, Journal of Abnormal and Social Psychology,* and *Sociometry.*

ARTICLES

Elliot Aronson and Judson Mills, "The Effect of Severity of Initiation on Liking for a Group," *Journal of Abnormal and Social Psychology*, 59, 1959, pp. 177-181. (The *Journal* will be referred to below as *JASP*.)

Kurt W. Back, "Influence Through Social Communication," *JASP*, 46, 1951, pp. 9-23.

Tom Burns, "The Reference of Conduct in Small Groups," *Human Relations*, 8, 1955, pp. 467-486.

Arthur R. Cohen, "Upward Communication in Experimentally Created Hierarchies," *Human Relations*, 11, 1958, pp. 41-53.

Leon Festinger and James M. Carlsmith, "Cognitive Consequences of Forced Compliance," *JASP*, 58, 1959, pp. 203-210.

Fred E. Fiedler, "Assumed Similarity Measures as Predictors of Team Effectiveness," *JASP*, 49, 1954, pp. 381-388.

Erving Goffman, "The Nature of Deference and Demeanor," *American Anthropologist*, 58, 1956, pp. 473-502.

Harold H. Kelley, "The Warm-Cold Variable in First Impressions of Persons," *Journal of Personality*, 18, 1950, pp. 431-439.

Harold H. Kelley and Edmund H. Volkart, "The Resistance to Change of Group-anchored Attitudes," *American Sociological Review*, 17, 1952, pp. 453-465.

Theodore M. Mills, "The Coalition Pattern in Three Person Groups," *American Sociological Review*, 19, 1954, pp. 657-667.

Irving Sarnoff and Philip G. Zimbardo, "Anxiety, Fear, and Social Affiliation," *JASP*, 62, 1961, pp. 356-363.

Alberta Engvall Siegel and Sidney Siegel, "Reference Groups, Membership Groups, and Attitude Change," *JASP*, 55, 1957, pp. 360-364.

Hans L. Zetterberg, "Compliant Actions," *Acta Sociologica*, 2, 1957, pp. 179-201.

BOOKS

Dorwin Cartwright and Alvin Zander (eds.), *Group Dynamics* (2d ed.; Evanston, Ill.: Row, Peterson, 1960).

A. Paul Hare, *Handbook of Small Group Research* (New York: The Free Press of Glencoe, 1962).

A. Paul Hare, Edgar F. Borgatta, and Robert F. Bales (eds.), *Small Groups* (New York: Knopf, 1955).

George C. Homans, *Social Behavior: Its Elementary Forms* (New York: Harcourt, 1961).

George C. Homans, *The Human Group* (New York: Harcourt, 1950).

Gardner Lindzey, *Handbook of Social Psychology* (Cambridge, Mass.: Addison-Wesley, 1954).

Ralph M. Stogdill, *Individual Behavior and Group Achievement* (New York: Oxford University Press, 1959).

Chapter 5

Interpretation, Prediction, and Control

The goal of each of us, whether layman or social scientist, is to improve our power to interpret behavior correctly in small groups, to predict events in them accurately, and to exercise control over what occurs in them. As members of groups we must act on the spot, but throughout this book two morals have been implied. First, we are better off with foresight than hindsight—better that we anticipate possible events than to wonder why we never thought of them. And second, we may be able to apply analysis in our groups when they are bogged down and cannot seem to get anywhere. Common sense and research agree that much group time is spent on activities only tangentially related to the group's tasks. If we think we are wasting our time anyway, why not try to analyze what is occurring in the group and why it is occurring? We probably have little to lose and we may have much to gain. The process of analysis involves giving and receiving help[1] and can be applied among members of a group as well as between members and outsiders, whether those outsiders be other laymen, professional consultants, or social scientists. Speculation and research findings provide sources for ideas and facts, and combining theory and research with giving

[1] See Warren G. Bennis, Kenneth D. Benne, and Robert Chin (eds.), *The Planning of Change* (New York: Holt, Rinehart and Winston, 1961), especially Chapters 4, 7, 8, 9, 11, and 12.

100

and receiving help may assist us in developing our skills in interpreting, predicting, and controlling behavior of members of groups.

What can be concluded about the study of small groups that has not already been said? How shall the preceding material be tied together and promising leads be indicated? Perhaps the first thing that can be said is to reiterate and amplify some earlier comments about the importance of studying small groups. If an individual were to keep a record of his daily activity, he would probably find that a good portion of it was spent as a member of some small group, either formal or informal. He is, perhaps, a member of a family, a car pool, a work group, a group of work peers, a committee, a bowling team, a lunch group, a golf foursome, a board of directors, and still others. Some of these small groups are tightly organized, others only loosely held together. Some are subparts of larger groups, others are autonomous. Some are very important to him, others unimportant. In some he is frustrated, in others he is satisfied.

What do all of these groups have in common? Primarily, they serve a mediating function[2] between people and the larger society of which they are a part. People contact the larger society and in turn are contacted by it primarily through the small group. The small group helps marshal a person's emotions and his knowledge and thus promotes action on his part. The help results because marshaling emotion and knowledge are partly dependent on experiential knowledge, and experiential knowledge is, as the name suggests, a function of shared experience. A citizen does not have to vote, and whether he will vote or not depends partly on whether he discusses the election with his wife, his friends, his coworkers, or others.[3] They may encourage or discourage his intention to vote, and may influence it one way or another. It is difficult for a person, alone, to influence the larger society, just as it is difficult

[2] Leonard Broom and Philip Selznick, *Sociology* (3d ed.; New York: Harper and Row, 1963), pp. 155-156.
[3] S. M. Lipset, P. F. Lazarsfeld, A. H. Barton, and J. Linz, "The Psychology of Voting: An Analysis of Political Behavior," in Gardner Lindzey, *Handbook of Social Psychology* (Cambridge, Mass.: Addison-Wesley, 1954).

for the larger society to mobilize a person's energies when he stands alone.

The small group also serves as a setting in which the interplay of personality and the social system are highlighted. Persons of diverse personality characteristics may find themselves performing the same role in similar (but not identical) ways, and society may find its normatively sanctioned roles performed in varying ways. An authoritarian person may be a democratic boss, and a society which values democratic leadership may have leaders who are, in practice, authoritarian. Which way the drift goes may be a function of certain conditions which are subject to control. Even though society may value cooperation and even though a man may prefer cooperative relations at work, if his job depends on his output relative to his coworkers then competition and not cooperation may be the result.

The small group may serve as a useful setting for research on some contemporary issues of importance. Current concerns with conformity and individuality are being enlightened through small-group research.[4] The nature and effects of pressure for conformity and the conditions under which a deviant person may develop, maintain, and express his individuality are being studied. The small group can exert a very potent pressure on the individual, but it can also sustain his uniqueness and protect him from arbitrary action. The increasing popularity of human-relations training and adult education, with their emphasis on the small (relatively speaking) group as the structure for work, testifies to the perceived importance of the small group.[5] Some researchers have imaginatively attempted to analyze international relations, cultural change, and similar concerns in a small-group laboratory, topics which are difficult to study in a field setting.

People may be impressed with the importance of the small

[4] S. E. Asch, "Studies of Independence and Conformity. A Minority of One Against a Unanimous Majority," *Psychological Monographs,* 70, No. 9, 1956; David Krech, Richard S. Crutchfield, and Egerton L. Ballachey, *Individual in Society* (New York: McGraw-Hill, 1962), pp. 504-529.

[5] See Bennis, Benne, and Chin, *op. cit.* in note 1.

group, but this impression will not mean much unless they are able to perceive events in small groups accurately and behave in appropriate ways. Although it is important to know about the history and background of a small group and its members, it is equally important to know about the "here and now" of behavior, about what is taking place in the immediate situation. People are often unaware of what is happening at a given time, and often their recollection of events is distorted so as to be more compatible with their beliefs.

It is necessary to pay close attention to commonplace, everyday behavior in order to focus on the here and now, on the immediate situation.[6] It is rather strange that people should resist the analysis of the commonplace so stringently since the commonplace is readily accessible and so obviously important. Staff members in human-relations conferences can testify at length to the difficulty in getting members of conference groups to look at the here and now of behavior, at what members of the group are doing and saying in the group at a given moment, not at what they did or said last week or last year or at what they will do or will say next week or next year. Even the social scientist engaged in research may avoid the here and now, finding it easier to take a few informants (or rely on his observations) and abstract and generalize in the direction of the ethos of a culture, the atmosphere of an organization, the cohesion of a group, or the character structure of a person: not this culture, or that group, or John Smith, but an ideal culture, or a typical group, or an average person. The acting person may also find it easier to be seduced by sweeping or curious or strange interpretations than to look at ongoing, manifest behavior. It is easier to accept or refute on emotional grounds than to think through agreement or disagreement.

A focus on the here and now also has possible consequences for the course of social relations. It is easier for a person to assume that he understands what another is saying, or that he cor-

---

[6] *Ibid.*, especially Matthew Miles, "The Training Group," pp. 716-725, and Philip E. Slater, "Displacement in Groups," pp. 725-736.

rectly interprets the other's intent, than to test the accuracy of
these assumptions. People don't have to interact much before they
have conceptions of each other, and they may then, acting on
these conceptions, find them corroborated. If an individual thinks
another dislikes him, and if he thinks the other person is a mili-
tant prohibitionist (and the individual is not), then he may give
the other good reason to dislike him by being hostile. But if he
finds out that, in fact, the other person likes him and is not a mili-
tant prohibitionist, then he has to reorient his approach to the
other person. The self-sustaining nature of social relations means
that people resist analyzing the here and now because they may
find out that their assumptions and beliefs about each other are
not true. If people find out that their assumptions about each
other are in error, trouble may be injected into their relationship.
Knowing too much may be as disruptive as knowing too little.

On the other hand, when people do focus on the here and now
they often find the experience rewarding. They discover they are
more alike than they thought (both presidents of large corporations and middle managers are insecure), and they discover that
behavior which they thought was capricious turns out to be
meaningful. Greater agreement on goals, values, norms, procedures, and role expectations may be discovered than was
thought to exist. Or, if less agreement is discovered, the basis for
disagreement is clearer than before. What seems to happen is
that the group's cohesion is increased or, at least, that its level
of cohesion becomes clearer. If a person has something to hide,
a focus on the here and now is a threat since it will be more difficult to avoid explaining his position.

A focus on the here and now may help understanding and may
promote desired objectives, but not always. Although some
things may be better said, other things may be better unsaid.
It may sometimes be wiser not to say what a person thinks or
suspects, even if the other person thinks or suspects the same
thing, if saying it would not be considered socially proper or
legitimate. The secretary may think the boss has designs on her,
and he may, but if she says so, she may lose her job or find it
difficult to avoid an affair.

It is probably true that most people err on the side of too little rather than too much communication. If a person tries to say what he thinks and feels, his sense of social appropriateness will probably keep him from communicating too much and the net result will be an increase in his involvement in the situation. Other members of the group will put direct or indirect pressure on him to make his contributions meaningful, but he will have to listen carefully to get his point in at the right time. As he listens and responds to the flow of influence, his assumptions and suspicions may be altered, and as he expresses his ideas and feelings, increased opportunity for consensus may be developed.

This introduction now gives over to a discussion of some topics under headings of interpretation, prediction, and control. Under *interpretation*, some of the ways in which a person may sensitize himself to important aspects of a small group will be highlighted. Interpretation will be discussed in terms of self-evaluation, diagnosis, and understanding. Under *prediction*, field studies, laboratory studies, and a combined field-laboratory design will be discussed. In addition, promising innovations in symbolic interaction theory and computer simulation as they bear on the field-laboratory distinctions will be mentioned. Finally, the topic of *control* will be taken up, and some of the ways in which a person may affect his participation in groups and the course of a group's life will be discussed.

INTERPRETATION

To interpret behavior correctly, the interpreter must diagnose and understand the behavior of others, but before he can do so he must evaluate himself—for until he has evaluated himself his personal qualities will almost certainly distort the observations and perceptions which enter into diagnosis and understanding. *Self-evaluation* is an exceedingly difficult art.[7] One's sense of

[7] Renato Tagiuri and Luigi Petrullo (eds.), *Person Perception and Interpersonal Behavior* (Stanford: Stanford University Press, 1958); Joachim Israel, *Self-Evaluation in Groups*, Stockholm Studies in Sociology, Vol. 1 (Stockholm: Almqvist and Wiksell, 1956); Tamotsu Shibutani, *Society and Personality* (Englewood Cliffs, N.J.: Prentice-Hall, 1961).

identity is complex, ranging from habit to the unconscious and being intricately tied together. Self-identity is a lifelong product and the result of numerous reformulations, additions, modifications, and deletions as the individual seeks to sustain his sense of self. Having achieved and maintained a sense of personal identity and, in so doing, having had to integrate incongruities, the individual is not likely to be willing, much less able, to take a dispassionate view of himself.

If a person is to penetrate beyond the interpretive power of the attitude of everyday life he must develop the ability to evaluate himself, to entertain possible interpretations of his behavior. He must be able to consider the possibility that his forgetfulness may mean, in addition to a faulty memory, lack of interest, anxiety, fear of failure, or the manifestation of a cultural expectation. In order to develop a self-evaluative attitude, a person needs a framework within which to lodge his interpretations. He needs some categories to stimulate him to consider different types of interpretations. One such framework may be derived from role theory and, since it focuses on personal objectives in an interpersonal relation, may serve as a useful framework.

A role may be considered a behavior system which has been internalized and developed for various purposes. This behavior system may be thought of as a strategy or set of strategies for a person to employ as he seeks to accomplish his objectives.[8] Some objectives are social and cultural; an individual's behavior in achieving them tends to be highly routine, and he acts in an unself-conscious manner. Routine, unself-conscious behavior may be most accessible to self-reflection since it is not likely to call forth defensive feelings. What is socially appropriate for an individual to do in a given situation is probably done with little conscious effort since it "comes naturally." But he may also, upon reflection, recall the nature of this behavior and entertain possible interpretations of it. He may come to realize that another

---

[8] See John W. Thibaut and Harold H. Kelley, *The Social Psychology of Groups* (New York: Wiley, 1959); Erving Goffman, *The Presentation of Self in Everyday Life* (Indianapolis: Bobbs-Merrill, 1961).

person's behavior is more a reflection of the other's subcultural background than of any conscious intent on the other's part.

Other objectives, however, are personal; an individual's behavior, in achieving them, tends to be self-conscious. Thus a person intends to do something or to create some impression and acts quite self-consciously in so doing. He is aware of what he is doing and of the objectives he hopes to accomplish, and is concerned to discover whether or not he has achieved them. This type of behavior is less accessible to self-evaluation but, since it is actively and consciously pursued, is still subject to some degree of self-awareness. A person may look back on a situation and admit to himself what he was up to, but, since some of his personal objectives may not be honorable, he is not too likely to share knowledge of these with others. And, since if they are not honorable he is not likely to admit them too readily even to himself, he may be more defensive about them than about his social objectives.

A third type of objective is characterological and a person's behavior, in this case, tends to be unconscious. The individual, unaware of the objectives he is pursuing, acts in ways of which he is unaware. And when he becomes aware of his behavior he is unable to interpret it, even to himself. His dominant feeling is confusion—he doesn't know why he did something, since he did not intend to do so and cannot imagine how he could possibly benefit from it. This type of behavior is least accessible to self-evaluation and an individual is most likely to deny its existence and to be defensive about it.

When objectives are not achieved and the individual has exhausted his role strategies, he may develop psychosomatic symptom responses as a device (probably not self-consciously applied) to deal with a situation. When the housewife cannot properly reject an invitation to a party, when her personal reasons for staying home are not accepted, and when her characterological behavior, if she were to go, would jeopardize other objectives (such as her husband's job security), then a splitting headache, nausea, or a sinus attack may ensue. And, since such a response successfully keeps her home, it may become a role strategy to employ under given circumstances.

Self-evaluation may be aided by entertaining the possibility of different objectives. It is necessary to keep in mind that all of these objectives or only one may be present in a given case, and that their possible existence may go far toward explaining the individual's behavior in a small group. The chairman may keep order in the discussion (a social objective); he may direct sarcastic remarks at Joe, a person he wants to silence (a personal objective); he may consistently misinterpret the remarks of Bill, a person he doesn't like (a characterological objective); and he may adjourn the meeting when it gets out of control on the grounds that his old war wound is acting up (a psychosomatic reaction). It will probably be easier for him to see that he maintained order but stifled suggestions than to see that his war wound acts up only when he is under stress. He may admit to himself that he was a bit sarcastic to Joe, but he will probably not know, much less understand, how and why he consistently misinterprets Bill.

One of the major difficulties with self-evaluation is that a person by himself finds it difficult to distinguish between what he thinks himself to be and what he manifests to others.[9] In an interpersonal situation each person must claim to be more than is apparent on the surface, and, for social life to be sustained, these claims must be honored. But the translation of intent into manifest behavior, and the interpretation by the other of the intent behind that manifest behavior, are fraught with distortion. How can one person convince others that he is honest and responsible? And how can others infer this promissory self from the existential self?[10] It is most frustrating for a person who

[9] See Shibutani, *Society and Personality, op. cit.* in note 7, especially Chapters 3, 4, 5, and 13.

[10] The distinction between a promissory self and an existential self is derived primarily from Alfred Schutz, "Common-Sense and Scientific Interpretation of Human Action," *Philosophy and Phenomenological Research*, 14, 1953, pp. 1-38; and "On Multiple Realities," *Philosophy and Phenomenological Research*, 5, 1945, pp. 533-575.

thinks of himself as warm and friendly to discover that others see him as cold and aloof. How can he modify this distortion between intent and perception? Thinking he was expressing what he felt, is he to conclude that he is somehow failing to emit cues of warmth and friendliness, or that others are misinterpreting his behavior? Unless he is able to find out how others perceive him, he is not likely to be aware of the difference between what he thinks he is and what he manifests to others. Thus self-evaluation can carry him only so far, and then he must rely on diagnosis.

Diagnosis draws on the arts of speculation and consultation. Somehow, interpretation must move beyond self-evaluation to an interpersonal evaluation. The art of consultation deals with this extension, highlighting emotionality[11] and problem solving.[12] The emphasis on emotionality and on interpersonal perception increases the awareness of distortions between intent and manifestation, and between manifestation and interpretation by others. It also increases the entertaining of interpretations stemming from personal and characterological objectives. The emphasis on problem solving injects a nonevaluative attitude into the interpretation process and helps both to reduce defensive reaction and to increase information.

Diagnosis may take place in a number of ways. An individual may consult with a friend who is not a member of a group, with a group member outside the group setting, or with other members in a group meeting. The group may develop a norm regarding diagnosis, calling it into play when the members cannot seem to get any place. However it is done, diagnosis adds a second dimension to interpretation by providing feedback, enabling a person to test his self-evaluation and his perceptions of others.

[11] See W. R. Bion, "Experiences in Groups," *Human Relations*, 1, 1948; Harold J. Leavitt, *Managerial Psychology* (Chicago: University of Chicago Press, 1958); and Warren G. Bennis, Kenneth D. Benne, and Robert Chin (eds.), *The Planning of Change* (New York: Holt, Rinehart and Winston, 1961).

[12] See Leavitt, and Bennis, Benne, and Chin, *op. cit.* in note 11.

Diagnosis, however, may be limited by the perspective of a group. An old and well demonstrated hypothesis is that ingroup cohesion and outgroup hostility are directly related. There are numerous illustrations of this hypothesis, from a boys' summer camp,[13] athletic rivalry, business competition, and international relations. It seems, often, that commitment to a group is developed and maintained partly by the satisfactions one gets from the group and partly by the perception of alternative membership groups as inferior if not undesirable. Prejudice for and prejudice against are both distortions from reality. Not only may group members' perceptions of themselves bias their ability to diagnose, but also their perceptions of others. For this reason, diagnosis may involve not only consultation of members with outsiders (to correct prejudice for), but also consultation of members with members of other groups (to correct prejudice against).

Self-evaluation and consultation can go far in aiding the process of interpretation. But they are limited by conceptual restriction and by the absence of tested knowledge. Expanding the imagery of members of groups requires excursion into theories of group behavior, just as increasing their awareness of tested knowledge requires familiarity with research findings. Familiarity with theory and research aids the *understanding* of behavior and, thus, completes the process of interpretation. If a person can evaluate his own behavior, consult with others about himself and about others, and understand the theories and research findings about small groups, he will go far toward a more adequate interpretation of behavior.

PREDICTION

The ultimate test of interpretation is prediction. It is relatively easy to understand something after it has happened, and even to delude oneself into thinking that he predicted what oc-

[13] M. Sherif and C. W. Sherif, *Groups in Harmony and Tension* (New York: Harper, 1953); M. Sherif, O. J. Harvey, B. J. White, W. R. Hood and C. W. Sherif, *Intergroup Conflict and Cooperation: The Robbers Cave Experiment* (Norman, Okla.: Institute of Group Relations, 1961).

curred. *Ex post facto* analysis is used but one always has the suspicion that such an interpretation is *ad hoc*. If the interpretation is valid, it should be able to stand the test of prediction. If it is a candidate for status as scientific knowledge its validity will rest heavily on predictive testing.

In everyday life, prediction suffers because people need to confirm what they expect. When confronted with disconfirmation, people typically reinterpret the situation so as to remove cognitive dissonance and to make their now remembered prediction consistent with the facts.[14] But in science, such a procedure is unforgivable. It is crucial to know whether a researcher made his analysis before (predictive) or after (*ex post facto*) he gathered his data and analyzed them. For this reason, negative findings and nonsignificant findings are valued. If a person discovers that he is wrong, and admits it, others can feel more certain that his hypotheses are predictions and not postdictions.

Prediction in human affairs is complicated by the nature of social life. These complications are not absolute, but relative, and their restrictive effect on research is gradually being reduced. The vitality of research in small groups is testimony to this trend, and some important concerns and promising leads are now becoming clearer.

It is useful to distinguish between three broad types of investigations: field studies, laboratory studies, and combined field-laboratory studies. A field study is basically a description of a small group in its natural setting. The researcher gains access to the group and observes it and/or administers tests to its members. Although he may make predictions of what he expects to find, more often he is concerned to immerse himself in the life of the group and to develop hypotheses interpreting its members' behavior. Thus his hypotheses are often postdictions and may be true only for this group. In a field study one is not limited to postdiction but it is difficult for the researcher to convince himself, much less others, that his data support or invali-

[14] Leon Festinger, Henry W. Riecken, Jr., and Stanley Schachter, *When Prophecy Fails* (Minneapolis: University of Minnesota Press, 1956).

date his predictions. One major reason for this difficulty is that the researcher has no control over the behavior of the group's members and, consequently, he may not be able to gather the data he needs or he may not know what effects unknown factors may have on what he does observe.

For these and other reasons field studies are primarily descriptive rather than analytic. Their purpose is to describe carefully and fully what can be observed and to use these descriptions as sources for predictions and as illustrations of propositions.

One of the best illustrative cases of a field study is reported by Homans on a group of working girls.[15] It is useful because the design, data, and analysis are quite simple and straightforward. In Homans's words, it ". . . can only be called a case study of the relations between repetitive work, individual behavior, and social organization in a clerical group." Ten women formed a group of "cash posters" in an accounting division of a company. Homans was introduced to them and spent about a month sitting at a table in the room where they worked, getting acquainted, learning the procedures, and gaining an impression of the general routines. He then systematically observed interaction among the ten women for fourteen days. Following this, the women were interviewed separately, along with their supervisors and other workers. From these data Homans provides a careful description of their job; their attitudes toward it, toward each other, and toward the company; and their social organization, emphasizing sociometric choices, interaction patterns, subgrouping, status, and personality vignettes. Homans uses these data to illustrate hypotheses and the conditions under which the hypotheses are modified (for example, the direct relationship between interaction and liking does not hold when one person has authority over the other). Homans clearly states that he is not testing hypotheses but hopes that the report will be sugges-

[15] George C. Homans, "The Cash Posters: A Study of a Group of Working Girls," *American Sociological Review,* 19, 1954, pp. 724-733; also see Homans, *Social Behavior: Its Elementary Forms* (New York: Harcourt, 1961), especially pp. 188-190.

tive to other researchers. He also hopes that the report will stimulate others to do similar studies.

As a model for a field study Homans's report is quite good. It demonstrates the method, the procedures, and the interpretive power of descriptive material. It is useful as a source for hypotheses and as illustrative material. Although it was limited as a predictive study, the general method could be applied predictively with one group, two groups, or several groups. Blau's analysis of a civil-service agency[16] is a good illustration of a field study involving prediction.

Such studies are important but are infrequently made. Their paucity is probably due in large part to the time involved and the tedious nature of observation. They are essential, however, if exciting and innovative leads are to be developed, and if laboratory studies are to avoid overly narrow specialization.

A laboratory study is a carefully controlled experiment conducted on a collection of persons who, for a brief period of time, function as a group. Because the researcher has control over most facets of the situation he can systematically analyze the relation among a limited number of variables. Thus he can systematically vary sentiment and observe the effects on interaction, or influence and observe the effects on conformity. He may vary the design to have small or large groups, similar or dissimilar members, few or many groups. He may also simulate groups by controlling interpersonal contact or by utilizing recorded messages. And, with the growing popularity and sophistication of computer simulation, he may even be able to simulate all the members of a group, include a great deal of their complexity, and analyze a complex set of variables.

For these and other reasons laboratory studies far outweigh field studies in quantity and, often, in quality. They make predictive designs not only possible but necessary, since descriptive

---

[16] Peter M. Blau, *The Dynamics of Bureaucracy* (Chicago: University of Chicago Press, 1955); also see Homans, *Social Behavior, op. cit.* in note 15, Chapter 17, which is devoted to a summary and discussion of Blau's book.

design in the laboratory would often be a waste of time.

A classic model of a laboratory study is Asch's research on conformity.[17] Asch (a social psychologist) theorized that people differ in their susceptibility to influence through suggestion, and that a perceived group norm would be conformed to even if wrong and even if contrary to their private judgment. Asch took a series of twenty cards and drew four lines on each card. One line was the criterion line; the other three lines differed in length, with one necessarily being closest in length to the criterion line. He then instructed three stooges to give certain responses to these cards. One subject at a time was brought into a room along with the three stooges, who, so far as the subject knew, were three other subjects. They were placed in chairs at a table with the subject on one end. The experimenter explained the task and procedure, which involved showing one card at a time and having the subjects, in sequence, indicate their choice of the line closest in length to the criterion line. The three stooges gave their choices first, the naive subject last. On the early cards the stooges gave differing responses, but on the later cards all three stooges gave the same response. Sometimes their response was correct, sometimes it was incorrect. The question was: would the subject perceive agreement by the other three as a group norm and, if so, would he give the same choice even when he otherwise might give another choice? The answer was yes, for most subjects, though some subjects would stick to their private judgment.

Basically, the design of Asch's study is simple, the task is easy, and the implications are profound. The experiment also lends itself to numerous modifications. What happens in the presence of only one stooge, of two stooges, or of more than three stooges? What happens when there are two or more naive subjects? How obvious does the incorrect choice have to be before even the most suggestible person would resist conformity? What would happen if the task were modified and made more ambiguous?

[17] Asch, *op. cit.* in note 4; Krech, Crutchfield, and Ballachey, *op. cit.* in note 4.

What would happen if the task were so altered as to involve matters of taste, such as which painting was the most pleasing or the best art? What would happen if the group had high or low cohesion, or made private judgments before verbal judgments, or discussed their opinions before they made their judgments? These and other modifications have been made and the findings reported. In addition, similar studies dealing with other aspects of small groups and interpersonal relations have been conducted.

A laboratory study has many advantages over a field study. But it also suffers a major disadvantage. The group in the laboratory is a contrived group brought together only long enough to engage in the assigned task. The findings may apply to people in laboratory settings but whether and how they apply to natural groups can be judged only by testing them in the field.

The laboratory study tells the researcher whether his interpretation is cogent, whether, with other things controlled, the relation he predicts occurs or not. But other things may not be controlled in a natural group. Some of these other things can be introduced into the laboratory setting, but others cannot be duplicated. In the end the researcher is forced back to the field, since what he is developing is a science of small-group behavior, and what he wishes to predict is not only behavior in the laboratory but also behavior in the natural setting.

The application of laboratory findings to natural settings is not easy, just as drawing on field findings for laboratory design is difficult. The conjoining of field and laboratory studies promises to offer the design for this linkage, and one of the best illustrations of the combined field-laboratory study is reported by Rosen and D'Andrade on a study of achievement motivation among boys aged nine, ten, and eleven.[18] Briefly, Rosen and D'Andrade selected forty boys from a larger group on the basis of various test scores and family characteristics. They contacted each family and arranged to visit the family in the home. Two

[18] Bernard C. Rosen and Roy D'Andrade, "The Psychosocial Origins of Achievement Motivation," *Sociometry*, 22, 1959, pp. 185-218.

researchers (a man and a woman) went to the home and asked the father, mother, and the boy to sit at a convenient table, usually in the kitchen. The boy was given a series of five tasks to engage in, and during the course of these tasks the researchers systematically observed the interaction among the three subjects, utilizing a category system modified after Bales's system. Stress was built into the situation by the nature of the tasks and by requests for parental participation in various ways.

The researchers carefully devised the experimental tasks so as to gather data to test the predictions which they made. Meeting in the home and utilizing a natural group, they were able to develop a great deal of descriptive material and to validate or invalidate their hypotheses. They found, basically, that boys with high achievement motivation had parents who were more competitive, more involved in the tasks, and took more pleasure in the activity; that fathers tended to emphasize independence training and mothers achievement training; and that mothers were more emotionally involved—all in comparison with parents of boys of low achievement motivation.

It seems reasonable to assume that most research on small groups will continue to be laboratory studies, since facilities and student subjects are readily accessible. Field studies have been encouraged for several years but few researchers conduct them. The field-laboratory study has been reported a few times in the literature but it is costly to conduct. Hopefully, field and field-laboratory studies will continue to be made, and if the recent revival of interest in symbolic interaction theory is more than a passing fad these studies may increase. In addition, the increased use of computers for the analysis of complex data may lead researchers out into the field again, since the computer's ability to analyze many variables offsets one of the major advantages of laboratory studies, namely the elimination of all but a few variables.

Regardless of the fate of field and field-laboratory studies, the serious student should consider conducting all three types. Field studies are a useful antidote to the tendency to overgeneralize laboratory findings and they provide the student with an invaluable sense of understanding which he cannot otherwise develop. Laboratory studies are a useful antidote to the tendency to overgeneralize field findings and to overlook certain possible relations. In either case the tendency to commit oneself to a "simple and sovereign" theory[19] is tempting, but application or testing in the other case helps avoid this fate.

Prediction must be tested both in the laboratory and in the field. Promising leads may be developed in either case, but their testing and their application must not only be rigorous but also be applicable to everyday life. The goal of small-group theory and research is to enable a person ". . . to be able . . . to read the signs that appear in the behavior (his own as well as others)—to diagnose accurately what is going on, predict where it is going, and how it will change if he takes a given action—all of this soon enough for him to intervene and try to change the course of events if he deems it desirable."[20]

CONTROL

Given all of this material—the attitudes of everyday life and of science, theory, research findings, interpretation and prediction—what principles can be stated to aid people in controlling the course of events in small groups?

The most obvious principles[21] have to do with participation. A constant, sensitive, sympathetic attention to what members are saying and doing is invaluable. In order to maintain it, a mem-

[19] The phrase "simple and sovereign" theory is borrowed from Gordon W. Allport, "The Historical Background of Modern Social Psychology," in Gardner Lindzey, *Handbook of Social Psychology* (Cambridge, Mass.: Addison-Wesley, 1954).

[20] Robert F. Bales, "Small-Group Theory and Research," in Robert K. Merton, Leonard Broom, and Leonard S. Cottrell, Jr. (eds.), *Sociology Today* (New York: Basic Books, 1959), p. 296.

[21] These principles are based primarily on: Bales, *op. cit.* in note 20; Bales, "In Conference," *Harvard Business Review*, 32, 1954; Bennis, Benne, and Chin, *op. cit.* in note 1, especially Chapters 11 and 12.

ber has to keep his eyes on the group, to talk to everyone, and to listen and react. Silence does not give consent except to the silent person—others may differ markedly in their interpretation of his silence. Eye contact communicates, as do other forms of nonverbal behavior.

It is also important for a member to be constantly aware of his own feelings and ideas and to express them when it is appropriate to do so. Being aware means a search for meaning. If a member feels angry, it is useful for him to recognize this emotion and also useful to try to figure out why he is angry. It may be useful to express this anger or it may not. This decision will rest on a prediction of what the effect will be, which in turn will partly depend on interpretations of others in the group.

Another set of principles deal with procedures. In a task group, the discussion normally moves from facts to feelings to action. Time must be allowed for questions and reactions, and when trouble occurs it is useful to try to clarify the problem by exploring disagreement or by backtracking to facts and direct experience. Norms governing procedure normally develop, and awareness of these norms helps toward the correct interpretation of the course of events.

The makeup of a group is also important. Similarity is an aid to developing cohesion; cohesion in turn is related to the success of a group. Homogeneity, however, can be detrimental if it results in the absence of stimulation. If all members are alike, they may have little to talk about, they may compete with each other, or they may all commit the same mistake. Variety is the spice of life in a group, so long as there is a basic core of similarity. Size has many consequences for a group. The optimum sizes seem to be from four to seven, with sizes five and seven having a slight edge by reason of the built-in impossibility of a stalemate—on a yes-no vote, there has to be a majority. When a group goes over seven, there is a tendency for subgrouping to occur and for some members to be silent because of conversational competition. When there are only two or three, power may become more important than the task. Analyses of the effects of size[22] have been made in the field in studies of committees, gangs, and other natural small groups, and in the laboratory, especially following up Simmel's discussion of the triad and the effects of the third person.

CONCLUSION

In order to understand what takes place in a small group it is necessary to focus on the here and now of behavior—to be perceptive of and sensitive to events as they take place. Perceptiveness and sensitivity will not carry a person very far, however, if he misinterprets what he sees. In order to interpret correctly it is necessary for a person to have a high degree of insight into himself. If he has a high degree of self-insight he is better able to diagnose events, drawing on theory and research findings and consulting with those whose behavior he is interpreting.

Within the attitude of daily life the test of the correctness of interpretations is plausibility. If an interpretation of events seems plausible, seems to make sense, then it is accepted as correct. As people become more informed by improving their self-insight and by self-consciously diagnosing events, their interpretations become more plausible.

Within the scientific attitude the test of the correctness of interpretations is causation. In order to test a causal interpretation it is necessary to predict what one expects to find and to control the effects of variables other than those involved in the prediction (or to be able to account for their effects). The development and test of causal interpretations is accomplished by field studies, by combined field-laboratory studies, and by experiments in the laboratory.

[22] See T. M. Mills, "Coalition Pattern in Three-Person Groups," *American Sociological Review*, 19, 1954, pp. 657-667; S. Stryker and G. Psathas, "Research on Coalitions in the Triad: Findings, Problems, and Strategy," *Sociometry*, 23, 1960, pp. 217-230; John James, "A Preliminary Study of the Size Determinant in Small Group Interaction," *American Sociological Review*, 16, 1951, pp. 474-477; Georg Simmel, "The Number of Members as Determining the Sociological Form of the Group," *American Journal of Sociology*, 8, 1902-03, pp. 1-46 and 158-196; Frederic M. Thrasher, *The Gang* (Chicago: University of Chicago Press, 1927).

Not all scientific research is causal research, however, and people in daily life do not ignore causation. A precondition for a predictive test of a causal hypothesis is thorough understanding of plausible interpretations, and much scientific research is directed toward increasing the fund of plausible interpretations. Such studies are usually described as case studies or descriptive studies. A precondition for correct plausible interpretations in daily life is awareness of research findings, both descriptive studies and analytic studies. The social scientist cannot afford to ignore the reasonable accounts people in daily life give of the events they observe and participate in, but, equally so, people in daily life who wish to expand their understanding of behavior cannot afford to ignore the findings of scientists, particularly when those findings touch on events in which people participate.

Selected Bibliography for Chapter 5

The topics of theory, research studies, and research methods have been covered in other chapters. The following bibliography is devoted to problems and procedures in the application of knowledge about small groups: a bibliography of applied social science.

Richard N. Adams and Jack J. Preiss (eds.), *Human Organization Research* (Homewood, Ill.: Dorsey Press, 1960). A collection of articles dealing with problems within a small group of researchers as they seek to carry out research, between researchers and the researched, on the roles of researchers and informants, and on various techniques of field research.

Chris Argyris, *Interpersonal Competence and Organizational Effectiveness* (Homewood, Ill.: Dorsey Press, 1962). A detailed report on the process of working with members of top management in one of the nation's large corporations to help improve their effectiveness, describing four steps in the process: diagnosis of the executive system, presentation of results of diagnosis to the top ten executives, planning and executing a "laboratory" program (sensitivity training), and an evaluation of the results.

Warren G. Bennis, Kenneth D. Benne, and Robert Chin (eds.), *The Planning of Change* (New York: Holt, Rinehart and Winston, 1961). A collection of articles dealing with four major aspects of change: social and cultural conditions underlying the need for change, conceptual tools for the change-agent, the influence process, and procedures for implementing change.

James V. Clark, *Education for the Use of Behavioral Science*, Industrial Relations Monograph No. 9 (Los Angeles: Institute of Industrial Relations, University of California, 1962). A discussion of the process through which a teacher helps his students learn how to apply the knowledge being developed in the behavioral (social) sciences, with special attention to the use of a laboratory procedure (sensitivity or T-group training).

Josephine Klein, *Working with Groups* (London: Hutchinson, 1961). A discussion of problems and procedures involved in working with various types of small groups, with special attention to the experiences of workers in Great Britain.

Matthew B. Miles, *Learning How to Work in Groups* (New York: Bureau of Publications, Teachers College, Columbia University, 1959). Similar to Klein, above, but with special attention to the experiences of workers in the United States and with emphasis on procedures of more direct application to educators.

Robert Tannenbaum, Irving R. Weschler, and Fred Massarik, *Leadership and Organization* (New York: McGraw-Hill, 1961). A collection of articles by the authors and associates, all members of the Human Relations Research Group, Institute of Industrial Relations, University of California, Los Angeles, describing theoretical approaches to behavior, reporting results of research, and describing problems and procedures in training to improve effectiveness. The appendix contains three critiques of the authors' approach, with special emphasis on the notion of sensitivity training, by Robert Dubin (an industrial sociologist), George R. Bach (a clinical psychologist), and Lyndall Urwick (a management theorist).

Appendix

Features of the
Successful Group

The following portrait of a successful group is provided in order to give the reader a model against which to assess his personal experiences and to indicate what the author feels is consistent with small-group theory and research. It is a descriptive (as opposed to analytic) model and embodies discussion of some of the problems which confront groups.

The model includes five features of groups. These five features do not exhaust all descriptive categories but they do serve the purpose here reasonably well. These features are objectives, role differentiation, values and norms, membership, and communication. The meaning of these terms will become clearer as they are discussed.

Objectives refers to the goals of a group, its purposes, its reasons for existence, the ends it seeks, or whatever other term one may wish to use. Generally a successful group has clear objectives, not vague ones, and the members of the group have personal objectives which are identical or compatible with the group's objectives. If the group's objectives are vague the members will probably be working at cross purposes since they are unlikely to have the same or compatible personal objectives. Consequently, the more time a group spends in developing agreement on clear objectives the less time it need spend in achieving them and the more likely the members' contributions will converge toward a solution.

Role differentiation refers to the clarity of the roles played by and expected of the members of the group, including whatever leadership roles exist. A successful group is one in which each member's role is clear and known to himself and to others in the group. It is also important that the official and unofficial leaders be known and that they function in ways to facilitate communication so that no member hesitates to contribute his ideas and feelings, and so that some degree of shared influence is present. The confusion when roles are unknown or unclear is obvious, but it is less obvious that the successful group is one in which role differentiation is clear and graded in terms of status and prestige. The popular notion that the democratic ideal is a group in which all members exert an equal amount of leadership may be a desirable ideology, but it has little support in research.

Values and norms deal, respectively, with the desirable and with the expected. A value is something desired or wanted by a person, something believed in. In everyday life a value is usually signified by one or more of the following verbs: believe, desire, wish, want, value, or prefer. A norm is a rule governing behavior, established and enforced by a group (or by some collectivity). Some of the verbs used in everyday life to denote a norm are: ought, should, must, or better.

Values, although an individual phenomenon and, hence, apt to differ among any collection of persons, are similar in at least some ways in a successful group. Having similar values may not (and probably does not) stem from members influencing each other, but from members discovering that they already hold some values in common. A group in which members do not share at least some relevant values is likely to be successful only for limited and short-run objectives. Though some differences in values may be present in a successful group, very little difference in norms can be tolerated. To be sure, some variation in general social norms is possible (people have different backgrounds and group affiliations), but the norms that develop in the group to govern the behavior of its members must be agreed upon. These group norms refer to procedure, including how decisions are to be made and implemented, as well as to the roles of the members. In a successful group these norms of various types are clear and agreed upon, and the group takes action through consensus, not through majority vote or minority railroading. Values and norms, though different, shade into each other at some point, especially when people try to justify a norm, since their justification often turns out to be that the norm is consistent with or contributes to some shared value.

Membership in a successful group is clearcut and members are heterogeneous. Clarity in membership criteria helps ensure continuity, commitment, and the development of group structure and process. Membership criteria, when made explicit, also involve attention to other features of the group, since at least some membership criteria will be relevant to the nature of the group's objectives, its values and norms, and its role differentiation. Heterogeneity in the group refers to diverse skills, experience, and interest, factors which will encourage role differentiation and flexibility in functioning. Few things destroy or incapacitate a group more than discontinuity or homogeneity in membership. Too much heterogeneity, however, may make it impossible to agree on shared values, much less accepted norms. Of course, a successful group can absorb some discontinuity—it will likely have to weather the loss of a member or two and the admittance of a newcomer or two.

Communication in a successful group is open and full. No one withholds relevant information, whether it be ideas or feelings, and each member provides that information when appropriate. In addition, at least some biographical information becomes shared, since open and full communication includes nonverbal as well as verbal responses. It is possible, of course, that some relevant information will be withheld, especially when disruptive consequences may occur. No husband tells his wife everything, nor do members of a successful group act solely on impulse. On the other hand, in a successful group no member withholds information because he is frightened, anxious, disgusted, or curious to see what will happen when he finally drops his bomb or quietly provides crucial information after the rest of the group has gone down some divergent path.

These five features, of course, do not exhaust relevant characteristics of groups. No mention has been made of cohesion, an admittedly important feature, nor of productivity, equally important. Cohesion and productivity are, in a sense, outcomes of a group. Cohesion is an internal product which, in a successful group, is likely to be high. Productivity is partly an external product, the contribution or output of a group, which is also likely to be high in a successful group. So, in effect, the above five features of a successful group are features of a group with high cohesion and high productivity. Or, to put it another way, the definition of a successful group is a group with high cohesion and high productivity, in which objectives, role differentiation, values and norms, and membership criteria are clear and agreed upon, and in which communication is open and full.

Finally, some mention must be made of another feature of groups, their autonomy—their degree of freedom from control or influence by other groups or persons. A group of high autonomy is apt to be a fairly successful group since there are few if any external forces maintaining it. If members do not have to be in the group, or the group need not exist, its very existence is some testimony to the presence of shared objectives and shared values and norms. Also, since no forces external to the group have organized it, whatever organization exists is likely to be a spontaneous, evolved product. This kind of origin means that the developing character of the group is considered desirable by the members if it continues to exist. On the other hand, a group of low autonomy is confronted at first with an organization—with objectives, roles, values and norms, membership criteria, and communication styles already established. But merely because they are established does not mean that they are understood or accepted by the group. Having them, a group of low autonomy can appear to be successful when, in fact, it is not.

Name Index

Adams, Richard N., 120
Allport, Gordon W., 117
Anderson, Alan R., 7
Argyle, Michael, 55
Argyris, Chris, 2, 3, 120
Aronson, Elliot, 98
Asch, S. E., 102, 114

Bach, George R., 1, 121
Back, Kurt W., 98
Bales, Robert F., 4, 7, 23, 27-36, 52, 54, 55, 57, 98, 117
Ballachey, Egerton L., 13, 102, 114
Barton, Allen H., 21, 101
Bavelas, Alex, 88, 89-90
Becker, Howard, 3
Benne, Kenneth D., 2, 57, 100, 102, 109, 117, 121
Bennis, Warren G., 2, 43, 48, 53, 57, 100, 102, 109, 117, 121
Berger, Peter L., 15, 16, 20, 62
Berne, Eric, 2
Bierstedt, Robert, 5, 59
Bion, W. R., 51-53, 109
Blau, Peter M., 43, 50-51, 69, 113
Borgatta, Edgar F., 4, 42, 57, 98
Broom, Leonard, 1, 7, 21, 27, 101, 117
Burns, Tom, 98

Carlsmith, James M., 98
Cartwright, Dorwin, 24, 27, 56, 57, 98
Cattell, R. B., 42
Chin, Robert, 2, 57, 100, 102, 109, 117, 121
Clark, James V., 121
Cohen, Arthur R., 98
Cook, Stuart W., 15
Cooley, Charles H., 20

Cottrell, Leonard S., Jr., 7, 21, 27, 42, 117
Cressey, Donald R., 2
Criswell, Joan H., 7
Crutchfield, Richard S., 13, 102, 114

Dalton, Melville, 70
D'Andrade, Roy, 115
Dentler, Robert A., 77, 78-79
Deutsch, Morton, 15, 56, 70, 71-72
Dewey, John, x, 50
Dubin, Robert, 121
Dunphy, Dexter, 32

Ellertson, Norris, 92-93
Erikson, Kai T., 77, 78-79

Faris, Ellsworth, 5
Festinger, Leon, 13, 16, 43, 47-48, 73, 111
Fiedler, Fred E., 98
Freud, Sigmund, 54

Gamson, William A., 4
Garfinkel, Harold, 9
Gerard, Harold B., 70, 71-72
Giddings, Franklin H., 59
Goffman, Erving, 3, 42, 43, 98, 106
Golembiewski, Robert T., 5, 56
Gouldner, Alvin W., 85
Gregory, Doris, 92-93

Hare, A. Paul, 1, 3, 4, 5, 57, 58, 98
Harvey, O. J., 110
Hemphill, John K., 42
Homans, George C., x, 23, 36-41, 42, 43-46, 47, 52, 54, 55, 57, 61, 81, 85, 96, 99, 112-113
Hood, W. R., 110
Hyman, Herbert, 15, 17

Israel, Joachim, 105

Jahoda, Marie, 15
James, John, 4, 119

Kaplan, Abraham, 19, 20
Kelley, Harold H., 42, 43, 46, 98, 106
Kelman, Herbert C., 43, 48-50
Klein, Josephine, 56, 121
Kluckhohn, Clyde, 17
Krech, David, 13, 102, 114

Lasswell, Harold D., 5, 7
Lazarsfeld, Paul F., 21, 101
Leavitt, Harold J., 13, 109
Leeper, R. W., 57
Lerner, Daniel, 5, 7
Lewin, Gertrud Weiss, 56
Lewin, Kurt, x, 23-27, 36, 47, 51, 54, 55, 56, 57, 73
Lindzey, Gardner, 36, 56, 57, 58, 99, 101, 117
Linz, J., 101
Lippitt, Ronald, 27
Lipset, S. M., 101

McBride, Dorothy, 92-93
Massarik, Fred, 121
Mead, George H., x, 20
Merton, Robert K., 7, 21, 27, 117
Meyer, H. J., 42
Miles, Matthew B., 103, 121
Mills, Judson, 98
Mills, Theodore M., 98, 119
Moore, Omar K., 7
Moreno, J. L., 60
Murphy, Gardner, 16

Newcomb, Theodore M., 61, 62, 63
Newman, James R., 19

Olmsted, Michael S., 5, 56

Parsons, Talcott, 57
Petrullo, Luigi, 10, 105
Philp, Hugh, 32
Preiss, Jack J., 120

Psathas, George, 119

Redfield, Robert, 5
Reichenbach, Hans, 16
Reisel, Jerome, 2
Riecken, Henry W., Jr., 16, 36, 57, 73, 111
Robinson, W. S., 21
Roseborough, Mary E., 58
Rosen, Bernard C., 115
Rosenberg, Morris, 21
Ross, Ralph, 15, 16, 20

Sarnoff, Irving, 98
Schachter, Stanley, 16, 73, 74, 75-76, 91, 92-93, 111
Schein, Edgar H., 2
Schutz, Alfred H., x, 9, 11, 13, 14, 15, 18, 20, 62, 108
Schutz, William C., 53
Selltiz, Claire, 15, 17
Selznick, Philip, 1, 101
Shepard, Herbert A., 43, 53
Sherif, C. W., 110
Sherif, M., 110
Shibutani, Tamotsu, 10, 11, 13, 105, 108
Shils, Edward A., 5, 7, 57
Siegel, Alberta Engvall, 98
Siegel, Sidney, 98
Simmel, Georg, 3, 119
Slater, Philip E., 65, 67-68, 69, 103
Snow, C. P., 8
Solomon, Herbert, 7
Stogdill, Ralph M., 99
Strodtbeck, Fred L., 7
Stryker, S., 119
Sullivan, Harry Stack, 54
Suppes, Patrick, 7

Taguiri, Renato, 10, 105
Tannenbaum, Robert, 121
Thibaut, John W., 42, 43, 46, 106
Thrasher, Frederic M., 8, 119
Turner, Ralph H., 10, 21

Urwick, Lyndall, 4, 121

Useem, Ruth H., 3

Volkart, Edmund H., 98
Volkman, Rita, 2

Weschler, Irving R., 2, 121
White, B. J., 110

Whyte, William Foote, 8, 81, 83-84, 85, 86-87

Zander, Alvin, 27, 56, 57, 98
Zetterberg, Hans, 21, 98
Zimbardo, Philip G., 98

Subject Index

Achievement motivation, 116
Activity, 37-41, 43, 44-45, 116
Attitude of daily life, 5, 9ff., 119-120
   multiple realities, 14
   personal perspective, 9, 10-11
   routinization, 9, 11-12
   stereotypes, 13, 60, 110
   typifications, 10, 12-13
Authority, 81-85, 112
Autonomy, 39, 53, 101, 125

Cognitive dissonance, 47-48, 73, 111
Cohesion, 25, 26, 33, 35, 51, 59, 85ff., 110, 118, 124-125
Communication, 5, 29, 31, 34-35, 65, 74, 103-105, 108, 118, 124
Compliance, 48-49
Conformity, 27, 41, 47-50, 59, 70ff., 102, 114
Consensus, 25, 32, 65
Cost, 42, 44-45, 46

Daily life, attitude of, 5, 9ff., 60, 110, 119-120
Decision-making, 26, 28
Deviants, 70ff., 102
Diagnosis, 109

Emotion, see Sentiments

Feelings, see Sentiments

Group goals, see Objectives, group

Hypotheses, 26-27, 38, 41, 44-45, 60-65, 67-68, 70, 72, 74-80, 82-84, 86-88, 90-96, 110, 112, 114

Identification, 49
Influence, 25, 26, 47-48, 53, 59, 65, 69, 74-77, 80, 91, 101, 114, 118

Interaction, 2, 3, 25, 26, 29, 38-41, 43, 46, 61-65, 112, 116
Internalization, 49-50

Leadership, 25, 35, 59, 66-67, 69, 81-85, 102

Motivation, 43, 44-45, 47-48, 66

Norms, 5, 25, 26, 41, 66, 70-73, 77-80, 91-94, 109, 114, 118, 123

Objectives:
   group, 5, 26, 122
   individual, 106-108

Participation, 34, 117
Personal understanding, x, 19, 102-105
Power, see Influence
Primary group, 5
Productivity, 25, 26, 59, 81, 85ff., 124-125
Proverbs, 17

Rank, see Status
Reference groups, 10-11, 70, 74, 80
Reward, 42, 44-45, 46
Role, 1, 5, 25, 26, 34-35, 41, 42-43, 62, 65-66, 69, 102, 106-108, 122-123

Satisfaction, 26, 32, 95-96
Scientific attitude, 5, 14ff., 119-120
   control, 100, 117ff.
   general perspective, 14-15
   interpretation, 100, 105ff.
   posture of doubt, 14, 15-17
   prediction, 17, 100, 110ff.
   theory, 23, 54-55

types of research studies, 111-117
typifications, 14, 18
vocabulary, 21
Self-esteem, 60-62
Self-evaluation, 105-109
Sensitivity-training group, *see* T-group
Sentiments, 3, 28, 31-32, 33-34, 38-41, 43, 44-45, 51-54, 60-65, 66-69, 80-81, 95, 112, 116, 118
Similarity-dissimilarity, 59ff.
Small group:
  basic problems of, 28, 34, 39-40

characteristics, 5, 66-69, 122-125
definition, 2, 4-5
function of, 101
size, 3, 4, 45, 118
structure, 3, 4
Social-comparison process, 47
Solidarity, *see* Cohesion
Status, 41, 45, 49, 50, 62, 66, 77, 80
Stratification, 51, 59-60, 69, 77

T-group, 2, 4

Values, *see* norms

DATE DUE

MAR 14 78	MAR 15 78		
FEB 20 '79	FEB 6 '79		
DEC 10 79	NOV 26 '79		
JUL 8 80	JUL 1 '80		
DEC 10 '81	DEC 7 '81		
8	JAN 2 3		
FEB 6 '85	JAN 2 3 1986		